The 2023 Rhysling Anthology

Also available from the

Science Fiction & Fantasy Poetry Association

The 2022 Rhysling Anthology
Edited by F. J. Bergmann & Brian U. Garrison

The 2021 Rhysling Anthology
Edited by Alessandro Manzetti

The 2020 Rhysling Anthology
Edited by David C. Kopaska-Merkel

The 2019 Rhysling Anthology
Edited by David C. Kopaska-Merkel

The 2018 Rhysling Anthology
Edited by Linda D. Addison

The 2017 Rhysling Anthology
Edited by David C. Kopaska-Merkel

The 2016 Rhysling Anthology
Edited by Charles Christian

The 2015 Rhysling Anthology
Edited by Rich Ristow

The 2014 Rhysling Anthology
Edited by Elizabeth R. McClellan

The 2013 Rhysling Anthology
Edited by John C. Mannone

The 2012 Rhysling Anthology
Edited by Lyn C. A. Gardner

The 2011 Rhysling Anthology
Edited by David Lunde

The Alchemy of Stars II: Rhysling Award Winners Showcase
Edited by Sandra J. Lindow

The Alchemy of Stars: Rhysling Award Winners Showcase
Edited by Roger Dutcher and Mike Allen

Order print or .pdf from **sfpoetry.com/rhysling.html**
or contact **sfpatreasurer@gmail.com**

The 2023 Rhysling Anthology

THE BEST SCIENCE-FICTION,
FANTASY AND HORROR
POETRY OF 2022

SELECTED BY THE
SCIENCE FICTION & FANTASY
POETRY ASSOCIATION

EDITED BY
Maxwell I. Gold

Editor and Rhysling Chair: Maxwell I. Gold
Book Design: F. J. Bergmann
Publisher: Science Fiction & Fantasy Poetry Association
SFPA President: Colleen Anderson

Cover image: *The Cosmic Heart of Speculative Poetry* by Dan Sauer

Cataloging-in-Publication Data

The 2023 Rhysling Anthology: the best science-fiction, fantasy, and horror poetry of 2022 selected by the Science Fiction & Fantasy Poetry Association; edited by Maxwell I. Gold

p. cm.
Includes bibliographical references.
ISBN: 979-8-9886318-0-4
1. Poetry. 2. Science fiction poetry. 3. Fantasy poetry. 4. Horror poetry.
I. Gold, Maxwell I.

For more information about the
Science Fiction & Fantasy Poetry Association,
visit **www.sfpoetry.com**

Editor's Note

The Cosmic Heart of Speculative Poetry

2022 was a truly spectacular year for speculative poetry. It's an understatement to say that we are living in a golden age of speculative fiction. The radiance which is defined by the spectrum of diverse poets, their styles, and genres—woven throughout this beautiful universe of speculative poetry, cannot be understated enough in this year's *Rhysling Anthology.* I'd also like to extend a special thanks to this year's Rhysling Jury and their diligent efforts and thank you to the Science Fiction & Fantasy Poetry Association for continuing to champion the voice of speculative poets.

This *Rhysling Anthology* would not be possible without the incredible work of our poets and those who sought to nominate them.

At the heart of it all is our poets whose passion, music, and spirit are forged into each line and phrase. To those who cherish these volumes, consider every poem in its entirety, and for its beauty and more importantly, regardless of what is or isn't subjective in the eyes of the reader; we would not have these treasured volumes without our poets.

From the bottom of this cosmic heart, thank you again, to the poets, for giving us the opportunity to showcase the brightest lights in our speculative firmament.

I'm pleased to present the 2023 *Rhysling Anthology.*

Maxwell I. Gold
2023 Rhysling Chair

Maxwell I. Gold is a Jewish American multiple-award-nominated author and prose poet who writes weird and cosmic fiction. His work has appeared in numerous anthologies and magazines including *Weird Tales Magazine, Space & Time Magazine, Spectral Realms, Startling Stories, Strange Horizons, Tales from OmniPark Anthology, Shadow Atlas: Dark Landscapes of the Americas* and many more. He's the author of the Elgin Award-nominated collection, *Oblivion in Flux: A Collection of Cyber Prose* from Crystal Lake Publishing. Maxwell has served as a judge for the HWA *Poetry Showcase* and currently serves on the Board of Trustees for the Horror Writers Association as the organization's treasurer.

About the Rhysling Jury

This year's *Rhysling Anthology* is the first of a new era. For the first time in our history, the Science Fiction & Fantasy Poetry Association is not printing every poem that was nominated for the Rhysling Award in the final anthology.

When we were a smaller organization, we could easily print every poem nominated in the annual book. Last year put us at a tipping point: the nearly 200 nominees created a book that was a beast to print, mail, and read. The growing interest in speculative poetry is exciting, but we had to find a way to keep the *Anthology* from growing out of control!

A jury for each category picked the finalists printed in this anthology from the long lists of nominees (listed in the back). Poems were presented without author names, and the two groups took their charge seriously to evaluate the merits of each work. Jurors separately evaluated a list of poet and publication names so they could indicate any conflicts of interest and recuse themselves where necessary. We appreciate their careful consideration as they selected these 50 short and 25 long poems to share.

Establishing a jury was not everybody's favorite option, and the award process will continue to evolve. But even with all the other flaws of any endeavor that seeks to find the "best," we are excited for another year of celebrating excellent speculative poetry.

2023 Rhysling Award Jurors

Short Poem Jurors:

Keech Ballard has been writing speculative fiction and poetry for forty years. In a previous life, he coined the term "transportation demand management," which continues to inspire and befuddle urban planners all around the world. He was awarded a Bank of America Achievement Award in Fine Arts fifty years ago. He recently sold a story to *Fantasy Magazine,* his first professional sale.

Roger Dutcher has been writing poetry for over fifty years. His poetry has appeared in numerous places including *Asimov's, Modern Haiku,* and *Northeast.* He co-founded *The Magazine of Speculative Poetry* with Mark Rich and edited it with Mark for many years. He was a poetry editor for *Strange Horizons* for almost ten years. His poem "Just Distance" won the Rhysling. With Mike Allen he edited *Alchemy of Stars,* an anthology of Rhysling winners.

Howard V. Hendrix is the author of six novels, around fifty short stories, and numerous essays. His poetry has appeared in many places, including *Abyss & Apex, Asimov's, Astropoetica, Eye to the Telescope, Mythic Delirium, Poetry Quarterly,* and *Star*Line.* His short poem "Bumbershoot" won the 2010 Dwarf Stars. His poem "Extravehicular Activity" appears in the April 2023 issue of *Scientific American* and "[is love that alters]" will appear in *Analog* in 2024. He taught at the college level for forty years and has authored or served as editor of several nonfiction books.

Diane Severson Mori is a professional classical singer and voice/singing teacher. Originally from Madison, Wisconsin, she has lived in several European countries and is now in the UK. She became involved with SpecPo in 2011 when she started podcasting poetry for *StarShipSofa.* She volunteers under many different SFPA hats, but most importantly as Membership Chair. She has edited, reviewed, and recorded speculative poetry in venues including *Eye to the Telescope, Amazing Stories,* and *Star*Line.* She has even published a poem or two and dares you to find them.

Ian Willey is a teacher, editor, and writer from Akron, Ohio, now living in Japan. He introduced the term convenience editing to the field of second language acquisition. He has published hundreds of haiku and senryu, including one in Japanese in the *Asahi Shimbun.* He began writing poems, prose poems, and flash fiction with a speculative element around 2019; his work has appeared in numerous journals including *Unbroken, Moon Park Review,* and *Mobius: The Journal of Social Change.* He was nominated for Pushcart and/or Best of the Net Prizes in 2019–2022.

Long Poem Jurors:

Casey Aimer holds a Poetry MFA from Texas State University and a Creative Writing BA from Texas A&M. He is currently finishing an MPS in Publishing at The George Washington University. During the day he works for AAAS publishing high-impact science research articles and by night he edits alongside his wife. He is co-founder and poetry editor of *Radon Journal* and previously published three full-length poetry books.

Bradley Earle Hoge's 2nd book of poetry, *N = R* fp x ne x fl x fi x fc x L (The Drake Equation)* was recently published by VRÆYDA Press. His first book, *Nebular Hypothesis,* was published by Cawing Crow Press in 2016. He has four chapbooks in print and his fifth, *A Human Lifetime,* is upcoming from Finishing Line Press. His poetry appears in numerous anthologies and journals, most recently in *Fault Zone: Reverse, Consilience, Eye to the Telescope,* and *Utopia Science Fiction.* He was the Managing Editor for *Dark Matter Journal.*

Tiffany Morris is a Mi'kmaw/settler writer of speculative fiction and poetry from Kjipuktuk (Halifax), Nova Scotia. She is the author of the horror poetry collection *Elegies of Rotting Stars* (Nictitating Books, 2022). Her work has appeared in *Uncanny, Nightmare Magazine,* and *Apex,* among others. She has an MA in English with a focus on Indigenous Futurisms. She is a member of SFPA and the Horror Writers Association, and her work has been nominated for Elgin, Rhysling, and Aurora Awards. Find her on twitter @tiffmorris or at **tiffmorris.com**

Michael H. Payne's novels have been published by Tor Books and Sofawolf Press, his short stories have appeared in *Asimov's,* the Writers of the Future collection, and 11 of the last 12 volumes of the *Sword and Sorceress* anthology, and his poems can be found in *Silver Blade, Star*Line,* and the *Civilized Beasts* anthology. After 15 years of posting daily comics to various websites, he's now settled into a more sedate rate of four pages a week while running SFWA's Featured Book program and compiling the monthly Round-Up for SFPA. Check **hyniof.com** for more details.

Amanda Worthington is the author of the self-published poetry volumes *All The Things I Was Not Taught* and *No Quarter.* She is the HWA's scholarship coordinator for 2023 and the founder of Horror in the Heartland, the Missouri/Kansas chapter of the HWA. A resident of Kansas City, Missouri, Amanda has had a long tenure as a public librarian. She served on the ALA's Best Fiction for Young Adults selection committee and routinely reads her work at spoken word events locally. She has been featured in Nina D'Arcangela's *Ladies of Horror* Flash poetry project. She can be found online at **theamandalaeffect.com**

About the Rhysling Awards

In 1978, Suzette Haden Elgin founded the Science Fiction Poetry Association (SFPA; "& Fantasy" was added to the organization's name in 2017), along with its two initial publications: the association's official journal, *Star*Line*, and the *Rhysling Anthology*, the voting instrument of the Rhysling Awards.

*Star*Line* began as a newsletter for poets with a shared interest in speculative poetry, from science fiction to high fantasy, from the macabre to straight science and associated genres such as surrealism, and is now a showcase for speculative poems and a venue for essays on speculative poetry and reviews of speculative poetry books.

The Rhysling Awards are named for the blind poet Rhysling in Robert A. Heinlein's story "The Green Hills of Earth." In real life, Apollo 15 astronauts named a crater near their landing site "Rhysling," which has since become its official name.

The *Rhysling Anthology* serves as not only a voting instrument for the Rhysling Awards, but also as a representative collection of some of the best speculative poetry of the preceding year. The nominees for each year's Rhysling Awards are selected by the SFPA members, who may each nominate one work in each of the two categories: Best Short Poem (1–49 lines) and Best Long Poem (50+ lines). All nominated works must have been first published during the preceding calendar year.

In 2023, as the number of nominees increased, a jury of volunteers was appointed to select the final candidates from the nominated poems. The Rhysling Awards are determined by vote of the SFPA membership from the selected works reprinted in the *Rhysling Anthology*, which allows the membership to consider the candidate poems without the necessity of obtaining all the diverse publications in which these poems first appeared. The *Rhysling Anthology* is also available to purchase in print or .pdf format by anyone interested in this unique compilation of verse from some of the finest speculative poets in the world; see **sfpoetry.com/rhysling.html** for more information.

The Rhysling Awards are currently the most prestigious recognition given for single poems in the field of speculative poetry. With each passing year, the number and breadth of the poems nominated, many by non-members and poets new to the *Anthology*, has grown.

Printing and distribution of the *Rhysling Anthology* are paid for by the SFPA. If you would like to contribute to the organization, so that we may continue to produce this and other publications, and fund the organization's efforts, please send a check, made out to SFPA, to:

Brian Garrison, SFPA Secretary
PO Box 1563
Alameda CA 94501
USA

or donate online via PayPal to **SFPAtreasurer@gmail.com**.

Donations to the 2023 Rhysling Endowment Fund

Benefactors

Kate Boyes
Timons Esaias
Mary Soon Lee
Richard Leis
Richard Novak

Sponsors

Jean-Paul Garnier
Risa Wolf

Supporters

Melanie Abrams
Linda D. Addison
Sharon Cote
Richard Magahiz
Miguel O. Mitchell
Vincent O'Connor (+)
Diane Severson
Benjamin Steinhurst

Donors

Susan C. Burke
Anna Cates
Robert Frazier
Mahaila Smith
Starship Sloane Publishing
Kyla Ward

Table of Contents

Editor's Note by Maxwell I. Gold, 2023 Rhysling Chair v
About the Rhysling Award Jury vii
2023 Rhysling Award Jurors viii
About the Rhysling Awards x
Donations to the 2023 Rhysling Anthology xi

Short Poems First Published in 2022 (50 poems)

Biophilia • Sarah Grey 3
Bitch Moon • Sarah Grey 4
Blå Jungfrun • Deborah L. Davitt 6
Black Pastoral: On Mars • Ariana Benson 7
Cassandra as Climate Scientist • Jeannine Hall Gailey 9
A Creation Myth • John C. Mannone 10
Dinner Plans with Baba Yaga • Stephanie M. Wytovich 11
The Epidemic of Shrink-Ray-Gun Violence Plaguing Our Schools Must End • Pedro Iniguez 13
Exulansis • Silvatiicus Riddle 14
Field Notes from the Anthropocene • Priya Chand 16
First Contact • Lisa Timpf 17
Fracking-lution • Linda D. Addison 18
The Gargoyle Watches the Rains End • Amelia Gorman 19
Gosh, It's Too Beautiful to Exist Briefly in a Parallel Planet • Nwuguru Chidiebere Sullivan 20
Harold and the Blood-Red Crayon • Jennifer Crow 21
If I Were Human • Marie Vibbert 22
In Stock Images of the Future, Everything is White • Terese Mason Pierre 23
Intergalactic Baba Yaga • Sandra Lindow 24
Jingwei Tries to Fill Up the Sea • Mary Soon Lee 25
Laws of Exponents • John Reinhart 26
Leda Goes to the Doctor • Pankaj Khemka 28
Lines to a Martian (Palabras a un habitante de Marte) • Alfonsina Storni, trans. Brittany Hause 30
The Long Night • Ryfkah 32
Medea leaves behind a letter • FJ Doucet 34

Mind Compression • Madhur Anand 35
Monitors • David C. Kopaska-Merkel & Kendall Evans 36
Near the end, your mother tells you she's been seeing someone • Shannon Connor Winward 37
Necklace • Carolyn Clink 38
New Planet • Kathy Bailey 40
Old Soldier, New Love • Vince Gotera 41
On the Limitations of Photographic Evidence in Fairyland • Nicole J. LeBoeuf 42
The Optics of Space Travel • Angela Acosta 43
Petrichor • Eva Papasoulioti 44
Pittsburgh Temporal Transfer Station • Alan Ira Gordon 45
Please Hold • Anna Remennik 46
Raft of the Medusa • Marge Simon 48
Regarding the Memory of Earth • Angela Acosta 49
Sabbatical Somewhere Warm • Elizabeth R. McClellan 51
Shipwrecked • Gretchen Tessmer 53
A Spell for Winning Your Personal Injury Lawsuit • Marsheila Rockwell 55
Status Transcript • Lee Murray 57
Strange Progeny • Bruce Boston 59
Tamales on Mars • Angela Acosta 60
Time Skip • Alyza Taguilaso 61
The Watcher on the Wall • Rebecca Bratten Weiss 62
We Don't Always Have to Toss Her in the Deep End • Jordan Hirsch 63
Werewolves in Space • Ruth Berman 65
What Electrons Read • Mary Soon Lee 67
What the Old Woman Knows • Melissa Ridley Elmes 68
What Wolves Read • Mary Soon Lee 69

Long Poems First Published in 2022 (25 poems)

The Bone Tree • Rebecca Buchanan 73
Corvidae • Sarah Cannavo 76
The Dead Palestinian Father • Rasha Abdulhadi 79
Debris • Deborah L. Davitt 81
EMDR • Marsheila Rockwell 84
ex-lovers & other ghosts • Herb Kauderer 86

field notes from an investigation into the self • Max Pasakorn 90
Georgia Clay Blood • Beatrice Winifred Iker 94
Herbaceous Citadel • Avra Margariti 97
How to Skin Your Wolf • G. E. Woods 99
Igbo Landing II • Akua Lezli Hope, Black Fire—This Time 102
Interdimensional Border Town • Lauren Scharhag 105
Living in Rubble • Gerri Leen 107
Machine (r)Evolution • Colleen Anderson 109
The Machines Had Accepted Me For So Long • Angel Leal 113
Matches • Rebecca Buchanan 115
Mouth of Mirrors • Maxwell I. Gold 118
My Great-Grandmother's House • Madalena Daleziou 120
From "Poem without Beginning or End" • Vivek Narayanan 123
Queen of Cups • Crystal Sidell 125
The River God Dreams of Death By Water • Ryu Ando 127
The Second Funeral • Kurt Newton 134
Spring, When I Met You (Spring, When I Woke) • Gerri Leen 136
The Thing About Stars • Avra Margariti 138
Who Came from the Woods • Lev Mirov 141

Acknowledgments 143
2023 Longlisted Poems 147
Rhysling Award Winners 1978–2022 151
How to Join SFPA 154

Short Poems First Published in 2022

Biophilia

I am alone. I have brought my phone to the forest
Where the cells serve none but each other, draw
No power beyond the reach of leaves for sky. Calls
Drop here, constant, caws and clicks and whoops
And warnings that my booted feet mar the mulch
With trails, with marks like fanned tails, like ferns.
I miss the message implied in howl and cry; although
I am similar in bone, in blood, I have enclosed my
Voice in lithium, I've bound my mind to counted bars
And I no longer comprehend the crunch of branches,
The scrape of brush, the rush of fur. Here I will open
A hole in the ground and place myself inside; bury all
Images and imaginings and lists and reminders and
All the songs I once called my own that were never, to
Begin with, mine. I will not sing but in the trickle of
Rain; I will no longer cry but to bring my loved ones
Close, to hold them safe. My only contacts shall be
Sunlight, treefall, decaying signals, shade.

—Sarah Grey

Bitch Moon

Here's a secret we small-town girls
don't spill: we've all been gutted
once. We've bled out in backwater
soil, our bodies bare as teeth. We've
worn our entrails like halos. We
chainsmoke our days to sear away
shame. We're a pack: share a
drag, shed our pain.

He's got a name

we don't speak. But we
feel it, raw as fever, a growl
like bloodstained gravel in our
throats. We rise like hackles. We
howl at the hard-choke approach
of his truck. We wait.

He's got a scent

we can sense on the
crosstown wind. New girl at his
side. New prize; new price of
living in a place where no one
minds when the next girl goes
missing, or comes home *changed*—
unclothed, broken, scarred and
enslaved to the fearful rhythm
of the moon. He parks. He
opens the door. We move.

He's got to *run.*

He's outnumbered. He knows
the paths through the hills like the
shape of our discarded bodies but
we've since grown fast. We outpace,
outflank. We snap at the boots that
kicked us down, gnaw the hands
that beat us. He shrieks for his

mother with a mouth
that called us
dogs.

He falls.

He bleeds out alone on an
unnamed street, wears his
bowels like a woven crown.

Distant, his new girl screams.

We keen to the moon
for this last woman
saved.

Then we right ourselves, light a
smoke, and sigh our secrets all
away.

—Sarah Grey

Blå Jungfrun

Do not take a stone from my shores;
don't you think
I can feel my own bones
no matter where they go?

I'll send my invisible sinews
after you,
threaded on the wind,
rise up out of the stone
you took as a mere souvenir
and teach you
the meaning of regret.

Bring my stones, my bones,
back to me;
leave them in the ritual lines
of the mazes your ancestors wrought,
the tattoo, the silent runes
that bind me here—

it's your best chance
as you sail back away over the waves
to whatever useless, silent land
you came from—
you'd best know
that I'm alive,
that I'm the witch herself,
not some feeble, fleeting human,
but the land, the earth.

You're adorable in your confusion,
your fear.
Come back.
I could just eat you up.

—Deborah L. Davitt

Black Pastoral: On Mars

i.

I was never much one for astronomy. My basic grasp of the universe
and its terrifying contents satisfied me most of my life. Pluto was a
planet then wasn't, then was again. I think I didn't go outside to
witness the eclipse because I've spent too many moons waiting for
obstacles to pass between my world and its light, for celestial corpses to
align. To call them 'bodies' implies life, and humans have long known
Earth only as a ghost.

//

But when I see that water has been found on Mars, I feel a knot that my
heart urges my tongue to curl into hope. I see life, blossoming bundles
of cells that compose Black bodies instead of confining them. I see
babies' tiny feet splashing in puddles from which their very existence
sprung I see water on Mars and know my children must never call
home by any other name.

ii.

Our backyard awash in desert rust, we'll fashion palaces
from red sand, all the while sipping tea sweetened with
spoonfuls of stardust. When winter rains turn craters
into ponds, we'll skate atop their frosted faces and in
summer laze in their pooled relief from the heat The
natal knowledge of how to swim having never fled a single
child's mind

//

They'll have a galaxy of nebulae to nightly gaze upon, eyes
bathed in cool slate absent scorching white sun Gravity
an alien bondage they'll play ball palm entire planets,
bound through the asteroid belt, swing from Saturn's rings
with their fingertips Astral amphibians, they'll breathe
purified pink sky through their skin Not a single gasp will
escape their grip

iii.

On Mars there are no guns   What good are bullets   that can be batted
down   like balloons   bleeding air?   My children will thrive   they'll
climb mountains only   to leap fearless from   the peaks   and drift back to
Mars   serene like leaves   in a crisp autumn breeze   colorful and   bright
and beautiful and whole   They will have all   of outer space to reach
their true peaks and drift   back to me. Colorful, bright, beautiful   whole

—Ariana Benson

Cassandra as Climate Scientist

Is tired of making graphs no one reads
or understands, tired of the tidepools
slipping away, the glaciers gliding
into oblivion. The way hurricanes
and wildfires take their toll,
but then people forget, rebuild.
Another night she sits
by the water, collecting
samples of phosphorescent algae,
listens to the seals bark.
The orcas rarely appear anymore.
In a library she leaves book after book
of meticulously collected data no
one cares about, pages never crinkled.
The dust in the library itself makes her
want to forget for a second about
migrations and the impacts of pollution
on gender in frog populations. She dreams
of slipping into the water, unnoticed,
of becoming a mermaid, a selkie,
a vestige between evolutions,
where no one can catch
or ignore her voice again.

—Jeannine Hall Gailey

A Creation Myth

This is how it all begins: the Cow is playing
fiddle when she jumps over the moon
while her fickle bull is left behind to work
the labyrinth. He's always on the run chasing

another 'brown cow' stuck in the maze.
But, Holy Cow, she keeps flying through
the heavenlies, clanging her bell with a spoon.
She stops for a moment at Lyra to strum

and sing a song of poems along with Jack
Horner (who's Jill he had left in the corner
of the universe). He sits alone minding his own
business eating his curds and whey

when along comes Miss Muffett who pulls out
a star, plum steals it away from the spider;
it is big & bright and sweeter than all the other
stars in the bowl.

Three blind mice balance on the black edge
of a hole full of green cheese and ham. They play
a violin too—the one they stole from the cat
who would pluck his own whiskers like a bass fiddle

until Mother Goose and Corvus the crow
both heckle and jeckle the feline as if the dog
days of summer aren't enough. The Cow
by now is feeling homesick and moos quite a bit,

but learns that she's home after all—she catches
the eye of Taurus the Bull, with his super big
red star that some will call Aldebaran.
He swoons and soon she gives birth

to many new stars and breast-feeds the dark
now gushing with light of the Milky Way.

—John C. Mannone

Dinner Plans with Baba Yaga

I tattoo a chicken's foot onto my thigh, your eye
a looking glass resting atop my bones. I walk on
broken acorns, braid my hair with the thread from
a lost boy's jacket. You scream from the pepper
plant growing on my porch, and I nod and nod,
agree with the spells pouring out of the earth.

I'll be sure to mind the roots,
collect the honey from the hives

You tell me to make a stew, to chop up the
onions, pull the radishes from the ground. I bite
my tongue, let my tears fall into the bowl, the salt
a sealant, a locked door boiling beneath the peas.
I stir clockwise to summon you, imagine the rancid
perfume of your ghost.

Yes, I have spiced the two-lips,
marinated the girl meat overnight

There's a routine to this, a ritual, the way
the kettle is forever on, screaming like a dying
red fox. I drink a broth made from feathers stewed
with baby teeth and sage, chop up potatoes
still covered in dirt, half-eaten by wireworms,
the taste of flea beetles still strong on my tongue.

I put the rhubarb on the table,
milk the snake over the sink

At nightfall, the scent of jasmine mixes
with the pine needles on the porch, cuts
through the musk of leftover promises
still lingering in the woods. If you listen closely,
there's a song in your soup, an alphabet
in your blood, each mouthful a child lost,
a child consumed.

I throw their clothes in the fire,
Eat their names under the light of the moon.

—Stephanie M. Wytovich

The Epidemic of Shrink-Ray-Gun Violence Plaguing Our Schools Must End

Their atoms dust the floors
of every school in the country;
those frightened children
we can no longer console.

Their cries have faded
into inaudible wavelengths
inside a quantum world where
hugs and spacetime both cease to exist.

They have dissolved into mere fractions
of their corporeal selves,
their particles swept into dustpans
and mopped into oblivion.

Blame those new blasters inundating the market,
stowed inside scores of scruffy backpacks;
the preferred choice of disgruntled
circuit-heads throughout the nation.

As parents, we stand before you
requesting prompt legislation to end
the rampant wave of shrink-ray-gun violence
endemic to our culture.

We beg you.
Think of the children,
screaming
beneath the soles of your shoes.

—Pedro Iniguez

Exulansis

> **ex·u·lan·sis** (n.): the tendency to give up trying to talk about an experience because others are unable to relate to it—whether through envy, pity, or simple foreignness.

I cannot tell you
of the shadows that rush onward
through the leaves in that moment before
they are taken by the wind.

Of the gods and ghosts that cut
through crowds like stalks of wheat in a field
and nudge me as we pass on the street.

I cannot tell you
of the strange women that live in the trees
whose eyes glow like distant fires
and whistle joyless bird-songs in the dead of night.

How the murmurations of springtide burst from the roots,
and with balmy wings run Jack Frost through,
rousing crocus and snowdrop in pelagic dance—
on sleeping garden–in iridescent swell,
waking hazy minds from languid winter dreams.

I cannot tell you, I cannot.
To be a child, chasing wild hares
barefoot through the grassland of an overgrown estate,
when, in stillness, you catch your breath,
and a statue moves to brush the hair from your eyes,
as field mice drop wreaths of tansy
and clover at your feet.

O, the muted madness I resign myself to;
the exquisite pain of an open heart.
I once beat my fists upon the doors of darkness
'til resistance bled me of banality
and truth, answering, gathered me from the step.

My voice rings now, as wind through leaves: is it not worth it?
To trade the mask of convention
for a dreamcoat darned with the heartstrings of magic,
and delicate patchwork—arresting wonder?

Can you hear this auspicious tithe of woven words,
peculiar legend without boon of a map?

I leave for you a gift—a golden apple
plucked from the low-sweeping boughs of the sun.
Taste it.
Arrange your doubts about the rim of your lips,
and chase the gilded sphere to the depths of your belly.
And as you burrow toward the center, does self not fold in upon self?
Inner and inner–the tighter the chrysalis,
the more brilliant the wings with which to fly.

I cannot tell you. In waking sleep, you merely forgot:
the golden apple is, after all,
the heart remembered.

—Silvatiicus Riddle

Field Notes from the Anthropocene

the dust of the empty streambed is
the dust of foxfur half-buried
in the dirt
jumbled hips and teeth and tail
jumbled acorns cracked open, waiting
for squirrels nibbling greasy meat
from overflowing trash cans
bags drifting among the algae
slime choking life from the edges
of the lake where shadowbirds
perch in trees and wail like cats
like children screaming for
belongings they were promised:
the trees in which they perch
are not the trees of their ancestors
but these roots dive the same depths
and the thousand fingers of fungus,
offspring of the last glacier's soil
have learned how to blossom in
hollows full of leaves that melt
in rain and crisp in pale ribbons
—a blaze set by light
refracted through plastic scraps,
the fading memory of
what it was like
when we knew fireflies

—Priya Chand

First Contact

It's a G.R. Blackwith work, you can tell
by the tiny, meticulous brush strokes—
greatest painter of the 2050s, and the subject
matter is clear—first contact.

But it's how he chose to depict that event
that's most of interest. His vantage point
must have been the hill overlooking the small valley
where it all transpired. Down below, pennants

in brilliant purple and orange and yellow
hang from improvised poles. Further back,
a slender silver spacecraft rests on rakish fins.
Smoke wafts up from a cauldron.

Three thin, long-legged figures tend the flames,
wispy orange hair in disarray. The Etcaelum,
they called themselves. Each of them has
their upper pair of arms folded loosely across their chest.

The lower set of arms they hold in front of them,
palms of their seven-fingered hands facing outward.
A trio of humans, clad in ceremonial dress,
approaches. The welcome party.

The precise moment of first contact. That's what
Blackwith captured here. Not the disaster that began
five minutes later, when the ship's solar array,
set for a world with a weaker sun, dumped energy,

a burst of power that ruptured plant cells and animals' eardrums,
caused birds to spiral from the sky, dead. Blackwith
painted the meeting, but not the catastrophic aftermath.
And never did. But what I see? He chose to depict

hope, not fear. So that we might remember the benefits
that came of that first contact. And it's up to each of us to decide
whether this painting reminds us of disaster, or the hope
that doors might open to wondrous places we did not know before.

—Lisa Timpf

Fracking-lution

Some things can not be ignored forever:
plastic bags pirouette on the tips
of tree branches, flags to all the
countries of needless consumption,
even when winter inevitably stripped leaves,
leaving the reformed polyethylene
swaying against blue sky, they didn't
notice, too busy continually buying as
the cycle of cold to warm to cold seasons,
night to day to night encouraged
their longing to get stuff, homes
filling with piles of useless things,
while trees continued collecting tattered remains
white green pink yellow black blue,
until one morning high-pitched
whining made them look up
to branch tips grasped by floating plastic babies
white green pink yellow black blue,
where plastic bags used to dance,
eyes unblinking, each mouth open
pouring strange sounds into windless air,
science had no equations to explain
the metamorphosis of reshaped fossil
fuel into strange life blooming above,
while at rivers & lakes they dropped their
rods in horror at creatures gnashing
on the end of their lines, no longer the
usual occasional plastic bottles, but
some Thing else....

—Linda D. Addison

The Gargoyle Watches the Rains End

not a thousand times like before, but once
… and slowly. how long until stone-on-stone

glass in his throat, a rasp, a strange friction
how he cracks when the field, cracks. cracks

when the hot winds blow, the red clouds gather
in bloom over a girl gathering dead lavender

below. oh for the drink he'd take if he'd known
the last rains were the last, oh for the spit

he'd loose. what good are his flippered fingers now
or his big O of a mouth? what good his short tapers

inside that spout, or the long neck that stretches
out to look at the girl and her basket and her thirst

in the dust of a sun going down? their thick tongues
missing water or wine, their afflictions tandem,

grapes crack on the vine. the iron bell echoes
like a thousand times before, and a dry moon rises.

—Amelia Gorman

Gosh, It's Too Beautiful to Exist Briefly in a Parallel Planet

In every scene from the alternate world
where skyscrapers are just inches away from
the ground,
curtailed by
the ever-growing Christmas trees, I'm a
good son,

& every mom thinks I arrived into my first morning
with enough motherly delight. I'm not going to
ruin their imagination, of course, what is the ruin
in telling the truth about
the machine
that we've now become;

a device whose cursor-hands point only to the
good reviews of the app from where
we hacked into this place? The point is: our cosmos is growing
into a bright castle,
almost into a milky world,
& to say that at least,
my mother is still my mother is the
only fact I owe you all.

The truth is:
she does not have

to bend into a ceramic plate to carry us beautifully, & my father
isn't the hand that will break her.

For the first time since 2080, we can all agree
that a god must not always beautify wreckage
to make it happen. At least, we've seen
to the end that there is—

ever-growing & humming,
it seems to browse us over again in
different engines.

—Nwuguru Chidiebere Sullivan

Harold and the Blood-Red Crayon

This tale has no happy ending, no return
to safe harbor and warm bed. Harold picked
the wrong crayon, color of gore, of living tissue
damaged and torn, and he drew nightmares
on the skin of the world until the point
of the crayon broke and the jagged edges
wore down, an old mountain
in miniature, a story told too often
as the corners of the book foxed away
to nothing. Now Harold whispers to half-asleep
children, reminding them that their parents
will die, their pets will die, the world will burn
and all the pictures, even the truest, reddest kind,
will vanish in ashes. He makes a line
between heaven and earth, sketches the curve
of a moon forever crescent, stuck behind
a leafless tree where a dragon has eaten
the last apple, and leaks flames from its nostrils
as it dreams of everything's end. Harold curls
in the scaly curve of its tail, and smiles.

—Jennifer Crow

If I Were Human

If I were human my thoughts would be
Chimerical sparks / reaching meat,
Memory [abstraction] written in
Acetylcholine, easily leaked:
Insert you > my childhood:
Misattributed dialog.

If I were human, my eyes ==
Blurry fat pixels [fix in software] &
Shredded collagen flecks
Darting / floating
Squeeze protein to focus;

My [backward] knees would be
cartilage accretions [un-kink]
My teeth of dentin with
crusty bits—I would
Decompose cellulous
> meat sack / midsection.

If I were human, a thousand
indignities & weaknesses would be
[me] but IF {
you would love me;
THEN I would love me;
}
Every pimple and burp.

—Marie Vibbert

In Stock Images of the Future, Everything Is White

I don't want flying cars. I want my language back.
I want to glass-bottom boat my way to a dirt road

with no street signs, squeeze myself on the grave
of my restlessness, my atomic self-esteem.

Five hundred years and we have finished. What
have burned sugar and dyed cotton blighted?

I stain my skin with sunlight, try on those
new underwater lungs, which is to say, I search

for new meaning in old salt. Sand dollars are dead,
I discover. I trade them for a tour ride round

the mountain. The cyborg guide has a tinny
Guyanese accent, points to a crashed, cracked

ship, which several Locals have adorned
with bougainvillea, flags and wooden beads.

The guide says, remember when the sky became
red? Look—how the giant stars came to us.

Someone beside me regrows their limb. I try,
but I'm stopping myself, and I want to go backward

in time immediately. There's another word
for lost, but I can't remember.

—Terese Mason Pierre

Intergalactic Baba Yaga

Chicken legs come naturally
to older women, but magic
takes vision, science, liminality,
and a certain homing impulse.
After vacationing as a short-order cook,
Baba Yaga mates her Chicken Hut
with a Tardis, and as immensity
enters it, the hut squawks,
immediately becoming pregnant
with intergalactic possibility
and unusual gestational changes:
booths becoming consoles, menus
morphing to map distortions
in the space-time continuum.

Always larger inside than outside,
(as all education is, Baba thinks),
the sleeker, stronger, shinier hut
now lays cobalt-blue eggs charged
with FTL potential, but maintaining
a chicken's peculiar talent
for finding traversable wormholes.
Early years of emotional starvation
have thinned Baba to a wiry integrity,
fitting her for quantum tunneling.
There is no stopping her now:
She embraces uncertainty
and goes where she wills.

—Sandra Lindow

Jingwei Tries to Fill Up the Sea

Mountain pebble gripped in her beak,
Jingwei flies over forest and field

mile after mile after mile, she flies
over rice farmers, over foresters

over river fishermen who spot her shadow
flying below them across a shadow sky

over mouse and rat, hare and shrew,
their thousand small and busy lives

mile after mile after mile, she flies
from the mountains to the Eastern Sea

mile on mile on mile to the shore's rush
where she drops the pebble into the sea

and the sea sighs, Jingwei, Jingwei,
you'll never fill me up with pebbles

and Jingwei fluffs her feathers and says,
pebble by pebble, I'll fetch a mountain—

I'll fetch a mountain to fill you up
so no little girl will ever drown in you

and the sea sighs, Jingwei, Jingwei,
children die, I'm larger than mountains

Jingwei turns on the wind, flies away,
back to the mountain to fetch a pebble

and the sea sighs but Jingwei has left
so the waves whisper to themselves

we held her, we held her, we held her
for a breath, then gifted her to the sky

and the sea shifts restless over sand
searching clouds for Jingwei's return.

—Mary Soon Lee

Laws of Exponents

So it happens like this.

New settlers arrive, they round up bricks from the prairie,
from the hills, from the valleys. Wild bricks.

These folks are new. They know nothing
about bricks. Many of the bricks
die in captivity. Die of malnutrition. Die

of enclosed spaces. Unwept. Sandy colored
bricks, red bricks, old chipped and worn bricks.
With utilitarian uniformity, survivors are piled
atop one another to form south-facing foundational walls.

Only the south. We don't build with bricks,
preferring to leave them to their natural ranges, living
in wooden huts and lean-tos. These new arrivals must be
transplanting some otherworldly practice that required
strong south walls, religious, superstitious, just plan practical -

they looked good the first year. As the bricks settled
in, got to know one another, then began fraternizing, marrying,
multiplying in the way that happens when you leave bricks alone,
suddenly the buildings began to shift. A year later, tipping.
By year three already some of the taller buildings fell north
as the bricks multiplied, the little ones growing to adulthood

in only a few months. By the fourth year, there wasn't a brick
building still standing, the bricks scampering into safety
in the woods or burrowing in sand. Since their various habits
had been so upended and new cultures transferred,
these new brick were unpredictable, forming new societies
with anarchic structures previous generations could only dream
or fear. The only colonizers left had moved in with us by then,

our little houses offering little comfort but stability.
In tidal world, the seas set the rules, but where no sea exists,
no one expects to find their very bones ruled by nature's quietest
citizens, the ones living in caves, in burrows, on tree branches.
These minute beings fall easily to our whims unless we recognize
that one is merely one part, one fraction of a multitude becoming

the future. Life is more powerful than those who live it,
each grain of sand a mountain waiting to be born.

—John Reinhart

Leda Goes to the Doctor

Medicine is magical and magical is all I think of

—Paul Simon

Like a slo-mo replay of an epic fumble
My M.A. plops yet another chart on my desk,
says, room one.

Forever practicing her modern hieroglyphics,
under "chief complaint" she's written,
"25 y/o O+ c/o N/V x 2 wks (+K9)"

Postman or doctor?
As a courtesy, I always knock twice
before entering the exam room

and for a fleeting second,
I'm startled to see a large white German
shepherd guarding the middle of the room.

The patient, malaised but not moribund,
perched atop the examining table,
says, down Zeus.

I introduce myself,
to both beauty and beast,
ask about her symptoms.

She says she's felt intermittently queasy
for a couple of weeks, mostly in the mornings,
but no diarrhea, abdominal pain, or fever.

Zeus's hackles rise
as I conduct my physical examination:
heart regular, lungs clear, abdomen soft, breasts slightly tender, trace ankle edema.

So I ask Leda about her menstrual periods—
she says, It's difficult to keep track,
I'm not always regular.

Then her eyes fly open—
she cries, Can't be, I haven't been with anyone
in a thousand years.

Just then, Zeus lets out a single bark—
as a slow blush creeps
up Leda's swan-like neck.

—Pankaj Khemka

Palabras a un habitante de Marte

¿Será verdad que existes sobre el rojo planeta,
Que, como yo, posees finas manos prehensiles,
Boca para la risa, corazón de poeta,
Y un alma administrada por los nervios sutiles?

Pero en tu mundo, acaso, ¿se yerguen las ciudades
Como sepulcros tristes? ¿Las asoló la espada?
¿Ya todo ha sido dicho? ¿Con tu planeta añades
A la Vasta Armonía otra copa vaciada?

Si eres como un terrestre, ¿qué podría importarme
Que tu señal de vida bajara a visitarme?
Busco una estirpe nueva a través de la altura.

Cuerpos hermosos, dueños del secreto celeste
De la dicha lograda. Mas si el tuyo no es éste,
Si todo se repite, ¡calla, triste criatura!

—Alfonsina Storni

Lines to a Martian

Could it be true that you exist, inhabit
that red world? That you, like me, possess
extremities fine-tuned to grip and grab at
things you need? A mouth that smiles? A chest

that hides a poet's heart? A soul suspended
from delicate, complex arrays of nerves?
Do cities rise like shrines to the lamented
dead across your planet, too, reserves

of youth and joy all drained like ours to dryness
by the sword? Has everything you say
been said before? Would the cosmos, minus
Mars, be emptier in any way?

If you resemble humankind so nearly,
why should I care if our worlds meet or not?
I star-search for a race that reads more clearly
the mystery of life, flawless in thought

and form. If that's not you—if you're no better
than us, poor creature!—don't answer this letter

—Alfonsina Storni, trans. Brittany Hause

The Long Night

The Winter Solstice is the time of ending and beginning, a powerful time—a time to contemplate your immortality.

—Frederick Lenz, Snowboarding Guru

In Earth's Northern Hemisphere
Our Great Mother labors through this winter solstice night
Daylight contracts to facilitate birth
Her Sun to be newly born upon dawn's break

But at today's early darkness
Neighborhoods shimmer amidst multi-hued light
Festive fairies flitter alongside seasonal cheer
In a twinkling
Nighttime conceals within crannies and closets

Afterward
As mere mortals augur immortality—
We toss out our Tarot cards
Walk the gateway to the sacred
Revel in the moment

Keeping fast our chinking bells
And bonging chimes
With votive candles in hand
Outside around homes, we parade

Our skin morphs in umber silhouette
In oneness, we emanate dark
Like the dead of night

Everyone inhales Mother's positive spirit

Nigh midnight
Piling pine, fir, juniper boughs
As merrymakers, we strike a cosmic bonfire
Bound by its fiery warmth
We gambol under a cloud-cloaked sky
And indulge in mulled hot cider with yule log cake

Even oracles clamor to cavort with us
Witches and wizards wave rainbows
Flutes, fiddles and pipes

Sound and surround our frolicking
Each person chants before the Great Mother
To assuage Her birthing pain through this long night
All terra's life delights in Mother's imminent miracle

In the wee hours, a full cold moon
Camouflages aback a lunar eclipse

At cockcrow
The Sun takes a first baby step
His light expands day after day
Via the summer solstice
But having kept vigilance over Her flourishing Sun
The Great Mother relaxes

Concurrently
In the Southern Hemisphere
Mother anew grows pregnant
Once again, She aspires for Her infant Sun's rebirth

—Ryfkah

Medea leaves behind a letter

Husband, the wise men in your city called me opportunist,
witch, foreigner. Of the three, this last condemned me
in their private court. Gave you permission to forget

that in my homeland I was called princess. How easily
you learned not to care that I burned it all down for you.
To call myself wife to you. Every woman, you told me

that last night in our bed, does the same when she marries.
Yes, Jason, in that you are finally right, and still
you cannot see the wrong of it. A pity for us,

I birthed only boys. Girls I might have left with you
when I burned it all down again. To share
my oppressive fate is less evil than to see sweet,

boy-baby faces, their copper curls silken under my hands,
metamorphose into patriarchs like their father. Better, then,
to lay my babies in tiny, boy-shaped graves, and
cleave the Athenian sky with chariots of grief and terror.

—FJ Doucet

Mind Compression (A Found Poem)

Every line of thought
is an oscillation we must enter
into arbitrarily

Only this small amount
of work in a vacuum
and it all makes sense

We are bound to equating
contradictions of experience
with experience

When a resonator tries
to communicate we should talk
about it, write about it

That famous incident
of the train, a collision
with the ponderable

The very special cases
they are present-day energy
they are light itself

Poem composed solely of words from Einstein, A. (1905). On a heuristic point of view about the creation and conversion of light. Ann. Physik. *17, 132 in:* The Old Quantum Theory *by D. Ter Haar, Pergamon Press, 1967*

—Madhur Anand

Monitors

Shana knew that many people
she met were aliens
in disguise: lizard people
who come from deep underground
bald Martians with retractable antennae
big-headed dwarfs from who knew where
but how to know who was who
and what was what?

Not only aliens: also A.I.s
Passing for human, mingling
With pedestrians in the shopping malls
Cunning artificial intelligences
Concealed in plain sight,
Their expressions somehow defiant
Beneath their Covid masks

What she needed was a litmus test
Of some kind, to define who was who
And what was what, and maybe even why
She needed a device to detect
these entities; she experimented
with parts from a metal detector
a smoke alarm, a Geiger counter
the completed device fit nicely
in the lacquered metal shell
of her re-assembled hair dryer

She tested her creation
but there was no response
until she showed it to her fiancé
its high-pitched whine pierced her heart—
she ran weeping to her parents
and the device activated once again
its volume rising as they moved
towards her, fixed smiles
plastered on their faces

—David C. Kopaska-Merkel & Kendall Evans

Near the end, your mother tells you she's been seeing someone

a lot of someones, actually. She doesn't know who, but they're
everywhere. A woman in the courtyard. Strange man in her room.

What? *Like people who aren't there?* "Yeah," she says, nodding
like she's not sure that's it at all. You press for details, waiting

for someone to bring her a chair after your long, unplanned walking tour
of the St. Francis parking garage, lost, somehow, though you've been seeing

a neurologist here for years. *Do you see any now?* She points to an empty
part of the corridor, where you see only a shadow. "A little boy." Never mind

that you'll learn, years later, your uncle died here, a curly-headed
three-year-old foaming at the lips. Little boys die everywhere, all the time.

You'll mention this to the nurse, and again to the attending. They'll run scans
that you'll save but never look at, the shrinking constellations of her brain

mapped too late to matter. The course is set now. This is already a ghost ship
but she'll give all the right answers. She knows the year and the president.

You'll tuck it away, one more weird thing to pull out and worry smooth later
like the black stone you gave her, in a little black pouch you'll find

in her glove compartment, still, after all these years and mini-vans later, because
you once warned her, *Keep it near you, always. That what makes the spell.*

The going gets rough here. You'll try to hold on, try to fix it, as you
were taught to do, but this was never you story to right, and like the ribbons

from your pigtails that you'll unearth at the back of her closet, you'll need it
more than you realize: proof that whatever it is that woman saw, she saw you, too.

—Shannon Connor Winward

Necklace

My necklace of strung bones,
some bleached and fragile,
some so new
blood and gristle
cling to them.

The smell is like daisies.

The necklace
warns the faithful—
stay away.

These bones are not mine.

I click through
my rosary
and remember each person
as they were before
I split them open
with some quick-witted
deception,
leaving them wondering
how they lost control.

Never trust me.

Never trust a woman
who wears bones, who
carries her memories
around her neck—
invisible, or not.

You are *not* listening to me.

From you, I will take
the hyoid bone, so all
you can do is listen.
Listen to the clacking
of bone on bone
as I recite my story.

In my youth, the bones were daisies,

yellow against my soft skin.
I dreamt my body would rest
in a grave brimming with flowers,
planted there by my children.
Instead, I trusted a man
who buried me secretly,
buried me in pieces,
scattered my bones.

I work my magic on you
and take the one chosen bone.

It is not my job to judge you,
your time will come.
I'm just another dead woman
assembling a body
bone by bone.

—Carolyn Clink

New Planet

There's a photo of my great-great-great-
great-grandmother
in front of Chimney Rock and a wagon;
she is holding a potato masher.
The metal cools her hand
as she stands in the hot sun
in my imagination as her great-great-great-
granddaughter hands me the photo.
The potato masher is in a
safety deposit box
in santa rosa california
Is it made of the same metal
as the box I am about to enter
in amargosa california?
How long will the masher's box
remain in place below sea level?
How long will my box last
hurtling toward mars?

—Kathy Bailey

Old Soldier, New Love

abecedarian

Aliens! Fought them when I was younger.
Bug hunt … that's what we used to say.
Carapace and stick legs, green ooze for blood.
Damned if they didn't just swarm all over us,
Every man jack, sometimes, and we would
Fire the lasers imbedded in our arms, full auto.
Giant cockroaches, six feet tall, chittering and
Hissing. The cybernetic mechavision and radar
Implanted in our foreheads used to light up
Just like fireworks within our freaking brains.
Killing, killing, killing … no end to it, it felt
Like. The war ended, strangely enough, with
Men, women, and aliens in diplomatic councils.
Never thought the damn bugs could even talk!
Over time, we were brought back to Earth, the
Prosthetic armaments extracted. The weird
Quiet in my brain then was unnerving: empty
Reverberations and echoes. I went crazy for
Some time … could not interact or even just
Talk with anybody. Every civilian felt to me
Unfamiliar, unknowable. Like aliens! I was
Very much alone till I met an amazing, lovely
Woman. Well, not exactly. Not a human, but a
Xenomorph. Like the enemy, back in the war!
You won't believe how smart and cute she is.
Zukola[*click*]mia, she's called. And I love her!

—Vince Gotera

On the Limitations of Photographic Evidence in Fairyland

Put down your camera.

The light here will not bend
to your command, nor dance with silver shoes
through mercury mist. It is no tame tiger,
and you are not its type.

Instead, you must court it
with subtlety and care, and it may deign
to accumulate for you in crystal glasses
as dew accumulates among the grasses:
Drink it down, intoxicating, deep.

Yes. Like that.

Now watch—it will perform for you,
watch it fill the fountains, watch them
fling it ever skyward, acrobatic, watch it glisten
on high-wires, sparkling, leaping from the towers

bursting into bright shards, rainbow-sharp

Don't flinch, porcupine. Stand still. Just let
the shrapnel pierce your lens. Instead of eyes,
a thousand glittering wounds henceforth to see
nothing less than glory and ephemera.

What human sight compares? No, you must stay.
Stay, dear guest. Be ours forever.

Stay.

Anyway, no one back home would believe you,
not with Photoshop and everything.

—Nicole J. LeBoeuf

The Optics of Space Travel

I descend from those who immigrated on ships,
the ones who crossed oceans, mountains, and borders,
passing through the threshold of space at escape velocity,
a Terran whose names reflect peoples encountered and lives lived.

Our eyes meet briefly as cloudy, stormy great-grandmother eyes
take me in, a child still learning to see the world in all its color.
In that moment she wishes a single glance could grace her descendants
with her decades of wisdom and travel plans for a new tomorrow.

Space travel is not a problem of triangulation and radio waves
as our space born kin gather in new types of ships, no longer tethered by gravity
but the optics of human life itself, the focal point between the past and future
through which a telescope points towards unborn generations.

My eyes are the bridge between worlds and generations,
when languages and cultures have been assimilated out of me.
I can still see the road ahead, of stories yet to be told,
onward towards Mars and the deceleration of the universe.

When my light goes out, the story will continue,
a new beginning shining on through passing millennia,
a taste of biological immortality not through cellular therapy,
but the stares and fleeting glances sparking emotions between us
that give us life and a reason to live.

—Angela Acosta

Petrichor

Ask me about my selves.
I can't promise to answer, remembering
becomes hard after you shutter
yourself in pieces to make room
for memory. The world becomes
the mind becomes a world where
knowledge is a forest, yet I still don't know
how many information it takes
to make a mind. I remember
rainy days, though.

Ask me about my URLs.
How the fragmentation of existence
bites immortality on the cheek and leaves
no traces. My cheeks are wet sometimes,
tears are salty; rain isn't, but one could
argue. What do you call a body
of water when it becomes rain
and exists everywhere?

Ask me about my death.
It was nothing memorable. I grew
old. I grew apart of me. Death
is a partial end. I keep existing in hundred
locations, seconds, years later and now,
here, talking with you, partially
a rainforest.

—Eva Papasoulioti

Pittsburgh Temporal Transfer Station

Main Concourse, 11:17 a.m., June 15, 2097

From the other side
of the surging time-traveling crowd
I see her with three other Girl
Scouts manning their cookie table.

I hobble over and lean on my cane
as our eyes meet and instinctively
she knows we're one (same as I
recall before on this day).

"I like your sparkly cane," she says.
"I know," I reply. "That's why
I finally bought it just last year."
And we both laugh.

I purchase a box of Samoas,
open it and chew on one slowly;
we just look at each other, our
eyes saying all that need to be said.

I turn as if to go but don't leave
just yet, waiting … waiting …
waiting … from this side and time
I know it's coming.

"Hey … me," she says softly.
I slowly pivot and face her,
eyes re-locking. "Tell me,"
she continues. "Did we do great things?"

I answer with a short barking
laugh, so integral to our being
that she has her clear answer.

And with unanticipated renewal
I march off to catch my time train.

—Alan Ira Gordon

Please Hold

Hello, our valued customer. Your call
Is vitally important. Your account
Is all we live for. Enter in the number
You're calling for, your date of birth. The day
Is young, the phone tree unexplored. We long
To serve you. Thank you. Welcome. Will you hold?

Thank you for holding. May we place on hold
Our valued you, our customer? (your call
Is too important to be rushed)—just long
Enough to transfer you. Now your account
Number, please, and then the joyous day
Of your nativity. And now the number

You're calling for. Your SSN. The number
Of glittering fishes that the sea can hold,
The grains of sand which measure out a day,
Stars in the sky. Yes, thank you for your call.
There seems to be a glitch with your account,
But don't worry, it won't take us long

To fix it—not when you reflect how long
Pines grow and glaciers crawl, the sheer number
Of years, by most conservative account,
That separate us from Earth's birth. Please hold
That thought in mind as we address your call.
We hope you're having a fantastic day!

Thank you for holding. Life is, like a day
In dead of winter, short, but art is long—
The art of customer support. Your call
Unfolding in five acts, the very number
The ancients recommend. Its tale will hold
A tragic flaw, catharsis.… Your account

Appears inactive. Yes, the same account
We have discussed with you four times today.
It is a mystery. But if you'll hold
We'll transfer you wherever you belong:

There're other worlds, and infinite in number,
And one of them is sure to take your call—

Your world. And you can call it to account.
Hold fast the day, the universe, your number.
Thank you for holding. It should not be long.

—Anna Remennik

Raft of the Medusa

The ghost of a French mariner visits Gericault's masterpiece

I appear before a painting in the Louvre,
a shipwreck at sea, framed as large as life,
with valiant seamen adrift and afraid
on a raft made from boards of their craft,
the lot of them weak and dying of thirst
with glazed eyes and burning skin,
half mad from drinking seawater
once the wine was gone.
I was among the few officers
striving to maintain order
while all the time fighting off the sharks,
then the damn gulls; days passed, until
with no hope of being rescued,
I tore the throat of a sailor close to death.

My teeth were strong, my need was great,
his fluids, balm to my parched lips.
Then straightaway, the other men
were fighting over his remains,
all but the African Jean Charles.
There he is, black as thunder,
balanced on a tilting keg,
waving his handkerchief
to draw a ship's attention.
All my days thereafter
I heard the moans of dying men,
tasted blood in the salty winds.
That crazy bastard got us through
but he couldn't save us from ourselves.

Inspired by the 1818–19 painting by Jean Louis Théodre Géricault, Le Radeau de la Méduse *(Musée du Louvre)*

—Marge Simon

Regarding the Memory of Earth

Composed by a Homo sapiens sapiens
1 AU from Sol in 2021 CE

In time, Rome will fall again.
New technologies will go beyond
our wildest dreams and nightmares.
English will require translation, and
tectonic plates will melt over our plastic mess
until: Pangea Proxima, mass extinction events,
Sol consuming terra, marching towards
the heat death of the universe.

Are there any voyagers left from spaceship Earth?
Will any wanderers read our inscriptions from the Milky Way?
When will our biological creations fail us? You,
in whatever time, space, or incarnated shape you exist,
will you remember our heroes and villains?

Answer me this:

Do you still close your eyes and recite the lord's prayer
before going into hypersleep at near light-speed?
Have you left literal milestones of our triumphs?
Can you hear the music of the heavenly spheres?

What will you call star systems no man has ever seen?
Or a sky so foreign even Polaris can't guide you?
Will you fear the impending blackness
as galaxies drift apart in an ever-expanding universe?

What will "Terra," "Luna," and "Sol" mean
to you twenty light-years away?
Have you taken poetry, art, the Popul Vuh
and the King James Bible?
Do you have an ansible or telepathy?
Has technology finally overtaken magic?

Are you happy?
Do you know of love and loss so great it knows no bounds?
Do you still dream in zero gravity?
Do you fear the space outside the airlock?

Science fiction has satisfied my thirst for your technology,
perhaps created from these very poems.
So all I want to know, all we ever want to know
facing the march of our mortal lives,
is if our progeny is still human.

—Angela Acosta

Sabbatical Somewhere Warm

after @notaleptic

change countries, an old friend
invites me to take a degree
in animal communication:

teach myself dolphin
go rogue with a wetsuit
train their gleeful saboteurs

pay for visits to SeaWorld
whisperchitter plans to
bored, angry gray bodies

take classes in underwater
welding, learn to breathe
from pearl divers, for

emergencies we'll create.
smell always of fish. offend
people on the bus. recruit

young idealists who learned
scuba with their rich parents.
so many things are vulnerable

to the sea: oil platforms, gill nets,
ships who still think dolphins are
charming good luck charms

toothy smiles in the monotonous blue,
not bombsmiths sifting supply in the
Pacific Garbage Patch. It makes the news

the day the parks show up empty,
no orcas, no grinning dolphins, no
laughing seals. conspiracy theories almost

immediately, millions of dollars
dried up like an arroyo, the
lawsuits. it is a sideshow:

it is a test. no one even guesses
except wide-eyed screamers lacking
credibility. the first oil rig explodes,

but the oily bloom doesn't rise
on the water. it is my sign to
bus down to the beach one last time,

walk backwards into the tide, fall
into the clustered warm gray and white,
joyfully renounce my citizenship in air.

—Elizabeth R. McClellan

Shipwrecked

sea girls are wrestling red tigerfish

while Margaret
gathers up
wet bones in a basket
with a howl
of wind blowing
cicada shade
through dank and damp corners
of deep-mouthed
ocean caves

her oars dip in and out of shallow water

the hot wheeze
of hazy, humid days
breathe in
breathe out
the bathwater tides
roll in
roll out

sailing by shore, she waves at white skeletons

in forced repose
some at tea
on sandy beaches
some reclining
in the jungle shade
all without clothes
(the sea girls claimed those)
wearing eerie smiles
under withering
sunshine
bleached
blanched
and dead-faced

... brave, it's important to be brave

while dredging up old friends
from watery, unmarked graves

—Gretchen Tessmer

A Spell for Winning Your Personal Injury Lawsuit

Wear beads of bloodstone and tiger's eye.

Light green candles.
It doesn't matter how many.

Pray to St. Expeditus.
You don't have to be Catholic.
        (It's probably better if you aren't.)

Google an image of the person who hit you and print it out.
Burn it in an abalone shell.
Toss the ashes to the north wind.
        (Check the Air Quality Index first.)

Do a Y/N Tarot reading.
Keep drawing cards until you get
        the Nine of Cups.
Ignore that it's reversed.

Bury a silver certificate under a new moon.
Dig it back up again when
        you're short on gas money.

Plant Witches' Herb under a full moon.
Harvest it when Mars is visible in the night sky.
Carry its leaves in your pocket.
Set some aside for Caprese salad.

Wish upon a star.
Not that one.

Eat black-eyed peas every night for a week.
It won't help, but you could use the extra fiber.

Fill a champagne glass with shiny new quarters.
Go outside and throw it against the gate
        in fury for all you've lost.
Then sweep up the mess, so no one gets cut.
        (Save the quarters.)

Put your disability check in a red envelope.
Sleep with it under your pillow for three nights.
Dream of what your life was like
        when you were whole.
Then deposit it and hope nothing bounced.

Gather the following:
        1/16 cup of pain meds
        1 tbsp of muscle relaxers
        Sleeping pills to taste
Grind them into a powder with your mortar and pestle.
Think about mixing it into your chai.
        Pour it down the drain instead.

Take a hot shower.
Weep. Scream.
Rinse. Repeat.

Hire a better lawyer.

—Marsheila Rockwell

Status Transcript

major, a set-back—
incubators are failing
on *Humanity* …

the project's other facets
proceeding as planned:
habitat and climate good

our sole vexation
is these damned incubators
vital for phase two

they still pulse yellow fluid
through ectopic ports,
they transfer blood and gas

and their outer skins
riddled red with thready veins
reveal the usual swelling

they're operational, yet
they're non-productive
for reasons undetermined

we've undertaken
invasive clinical tests
to find the error

results are inconclusive
we don't understand
the men's morale is falling

and existing crew
lack the coding expertise
to reboot the tech

as for the *Lysistrata*
when we forced the ports
the units self-destructed

though some will still blink
their viability is
poor in the long-term

the context just doesn't suit
we're lost without them
sir, for *Humanity*'s sake

we ask permission
to abort the colony

—await your response

—Lee Murray

Strange Progeny

Abducted by aliens
twice in my youth,
I grew up with
a life very strange.
Unearthly implants
lodged in my flesh,
yet few that would
buy my strange tales.

I married a woman
much like myself,
she was strange in
her own special way.
For she was a witch
and the daughter of one,
a lineage that traced
back to a medieval age.

Our children are strange,
of that we are sure.
They have special powers
I dare not reveal.
We fear that their lives
will be vile and harsh
in a world that can
only view them as freaks.

So I watch the night sky
and pray for some ship
to salvage our lives
in a miracle flight.
Across stellar space
to a world that is strange
and welcomes our kind.
Beyond the uncaring Earth.

—Bruce Boston

Tamales on Mars

The dry dirt of Mars could be
the deserts of Chihuahua,
Bolivian salt flats
or the frigid Patagonian steppe.

Here, my *bisabuela*'s recipes
can find new homes
with ingredients harvested
and cooked underground.

Pottery wheels hum in time
with the wind, birthing
new cooking vessels
with gritty, red stoneware.

We make tamales on Sundays,
filling them with the sweets
of dried fruits left in the sun
and cheeses from goats happily
jumping in Martian gravity.

The taste compares to terran delights.
We eat tamales and protein-rich beans
around a roaring fire where colonists
tell stories of skies of blue
and arid deserts like these.

—Angela Acosta

Time Skip

Let X be a gash in the fabric
of time that splits to show
things sixty-six million years
past. Let Y be the sea, rising
and dipping, sloshing sediment
and skeleton alike into chalk.
Let the chalk scry a spell of protection
into stone, surpassing all elixirs concocted
by modern alchemy. Let Z be the asteroid slipping
into sleeve of space—dark tunnel
towards tomorrow and yesterday
distorting history. Let our limbs bloom
poison and pollen like the first bees born into a world
without sunlight. Let what was written turn
to air—sulfur and carbonate filling the skies
for hundreds of years. Let the dinosaurs die
only after they have smashed these skyscrapers
into smithereens. Let the quake restrain
the epicenter of its desire to burst
as the universe grows larger than itself. Let sirens
find all the audible wavelengths
for sorrow. Let this small, blue world turn, tip, and swerve
beyond its predicted orbit. Let the stars misalign
in all planetary houses. Let the ghosts sigh
in Morse code and floating teacups
for another message misheard. Let predators consume
all these faulty human yearnings for money and more
time, all these things we pile up
gathering dust. Let the moon pull the ocean
to blanket these cold, barren cities. Let time skip:
favorite cassette tape on loop, vinyl melting
in a volcanic apocalypse, repeat
until the end. Let me listen
to the song of your voice in low fidelity,
warbled chorus of wishes—
ears, lips, eyes, all my bones burning
from this beating in my chest.

—Alyza Taguilaso

The Watcher on the Wall

Lured by the first snow of winter,
my dead father managed to struggle out
of his grave on the far hill, managed to stagger
down into the walnut grove to meet me
as the heavy flakes fell.
He did not look bad. There
was a grandeur in his features in the half-light of
my torch.
What is it the snow does for the soil, again?
he asked me. Fixes nitrogen, I answered. No, wait
that's lightning. I couldn't remember what the snow
does except for cover the soil, cover us, cover the
living and the dead.
My father looked at me with some pity.
I saw then how his flesh had fallen away, how
his farm clothes were tattered.
I still know more than you do, girl, he said.
I am the watcher on the wall.
Before he died he'd said that,
called himself the watcher on the wall,
and it had meant only
that he watched men in bad suits on TV,
and read prophecies about the world's end.
It had been an old man's fantasy,
his final dodging of the truth.
Now I saw that he had found his wall.
His eyes were visionary, at last. Whatever it is
that's coming for us, he'd seen it.
He opened his mouth to tell and I saw the blue
of bones and
the snow came between us and our voices
were silenced, and he could give no warning.

—Rebecca Bratten Weiss

We Don't Always Have to Toss Her in the Deep End

What if when she drowns
she grows gills
sprouting out of her hands
because keeping them busy
has always been
what's allowed her
to breathe?

She'll sink down
to the depths,
into what was supposed to
kill her, an environment
unsuitable for life, and
she'll live anyway.

Kicking stronger in the current
than she's ever kicked before.
The sea salt burning and
cleansing her wounds: the ones that
slice her arms, her legs,
her torso, her breasts.
The ones the world gave her
when she said,
"I am me."

Her eyes will begin to see
in the dark, light
filtered down, down,
down enough to make out
shapes and the half-truths
that drifted down with her from
the land up above.

Her eyes will adjust.
Her eyes will adjust.

What if her hair grows long,
like in all those stories

she's read, flowing behind her,
interlaced with shells and pretty
stones rounded smooth
on the sea bed?

Will we say she's beautiful?
Will we say she's strong?
Will we say she's thrived
given her circumstances?

Will we forget it was us
who threw her overboard?

—Jordan Hirsch

Werewolves in Space

I. Nearside Luna

When the full Earth rises
In the Moon's black sky
Earthshine's albedo
Isn't bright enough
To bring out fur.

Strolling werewolves
Walk unchanging on Tranquility
Human-footed over
The level darkness
Of the Lunar Sea.

II. Farside Luna

When they volunteer for duty
On a station in selenosynchronous orbit
Over the far side of the Moon
Having run across too many references
To that as the dark side

And thinking to be safe from were-ing
They're in for a grim surprise
At the mid-month fullness
Of sunlight rising
From the far lunar ground beneath them.

III. Mars

Even rising full together
Deimos and Phobos
So small compared to their world—
You'll be lucky if you turn
To a Chihuahua.

IV. Visible Moons

There's a full moon
Visible somewhere
Anywhere in space—
Probably a whole bunch
Of satellites to something—

But most places
If you're thinking
Of wolving it full-time
You'll need a heavy-duty
Telescope to see them.

—Ruth Berman

What Electrons Read

Notes from fellow anarchists:
how to speed faster than light
in a dielectric medium

reports of attempts to defy
the Pauli exclusion principle.
No success thus far.

Anything that admits
a multiplicity of meaning:
metaphor, symbolism, allegory

embracing the ambiguity
of their own plurality.
Particle. Wave. Mystic.

The Relativity Times:
scouring the social column
for news of the lepton clan

lingering over the obituary
of another young luminary
annihilated by a positron.

—Mary Soon Lee

What the Old Woman Knows

The anatomy of a fairy tale is inexorable
And here's how it goes:

I'm dragged from my quiet cottage in the woods
To Court, displayed like yesterday's stale baked goods.

Everyone falls over themself to believe
The ingenue's account of events

And by the time she's told her tale
And the man in the room—a king, a prince—has spoken

The situation explained to satisfaction
Through her eyewitness and his brave corroboration

All the air is gone from the space
And with it any hope for my salvation.

No one sees the Old Woman.
No one heeds when she speaks.

No one cares if she's innocent
And no one mourns when she burns.

Her body dissolves into the bad dreams of children
And her voice floats away like cobwebs into The End.

—Melissa Ridley Elmes

What Wolves Read

The posture of packmates:
ears, tail, stance, glance.

Traces of prospective prey:
spoor, scent, scuffle, scratch.

Paths to the spirit world:
wind, water, wolf star, moon.

When a path opens, they howl
at wraiths they cannot touch:

lost ancestors loping soundless
across a shadow grassland

cowboys slouched in the saddle,
women with babies on their back

and buffalo, unnumbered buffalo,
broad-backed, bounteous, toothsome

huge herds flowing like rivers
to some far and sundered sea.

—Mary Soon Lee

Long Poems First Published in 2022

The Bone Tree

There is a tree
that grows in the
woods at the heart
of the world. This

is not a tree
of wood, nor of
stone or metal,
but a tree of

bones. And the bones
sing, and every
day the tree grows,
for every day

new bones appear,
burnt and broken,
branching out from
its trunk, clicking

and clacking in
the wind that blows
through the woods at
the heart of the

world. And the wind
carries that song
across mountains
and deserts, through

cities and towns
and temples and
towers. And you
can hear that song,

not when you are
quiet and still,
but when you are
loud and angry.

The bone tree knows
your anger, your
pain, your rage, for
that is the song

of the tree, and
it sings with you.
It sings of wives
burned for husbands'

honor, children
beaten and locked
away, or forced
out into the

cold because they
loved the wrong way,
dressed the wrong way,
called themselves by

the wrong name or
were born into
the wrong body.
The bones of the

tree are burnt and
broken, for they
have been tied to
stakes and hung from

ropes, they have been
dragged until they
shattered, and crushed
under rocks and

earth, and tossed from
among the clouds
to smash against
the water far

below. Listen,
as you shout and
you rage and you
march, for there is

a tree of bones
that grows in the
woods at the heart
of the world, and

it is singing.

—Rebecca Buchanan

Corvidae

1.
She watches the ravens every day as
she leaves to walk to work (there's so many—
she never paid them much mind before he came
along), seeking one among the others, sleek

winged thing black as a moonless night, as
the gulf left in space when a dying star
finally collapses in on itself. She likes to think
she can tell hers apart from the others—

that one, cocking its head so like he does
when she's said something to amuse him,
obsidian beak unable to replicate the dark arc
of his smile, or maybe that one, carrying

itself with the same grace he displays standing
or dancing or bearing her to bed—that her eyes
are clever enough to pick a trait that unravels
the trick, but she knows she probably can't.

2.
Some days he perches on the telephone pole
across the street from her house and watches
her leave—slim thing, curls pale as young

wheat, eyes green as sea-glass; some
days he settles on a rooftop and gazes down
on her progress through the city's cracked

streets while a faintly smoke-scented breeze
ruffles his feathers. But no matter where he
sits he sees her, and he smiles because her

need is written so nakedly in every aspect
of her, her eyes so clearly seeking something
as she scurries through the concrete warren

she's made her home—seeking him. Her
ache reaches him above the static chatter
of every other mortal's longings, stirs urges

that keep him in this realm long after he
would usually have flown far beyond it—a
beautiful hunger, a raven's love.

3.

Later. The tap at the window she leaps up
to answer, feet flying across the floor fast as

wings eat up the sky; the scrap of shadow
that flutters in and resolves into her lover,

hair like ink splashed against his paper-pale
skin, lithe limbs carved from marble and eyes

of emerald; the smile at which she starts to
melt—and perhaps it's this softening that

ensures they fit together so well when he takes
her in his arms, or perhaps it's that their

forms, their souls, were sculpted by greater
and distant hands and subtly nudged, shifted,

positioned so they would wind up here,
together in every sense, within the improbable,

infinite mass of stardust and chaos that
the cosmos is—perhaps, but as his lips

brush her neck, as their fingers entwine on
her pillows, the cause has less meaning than

the effect, plan and purpose never pondered
as the moon makes her slow way through the sky.

Afterwards she beams with pride and says,
"I figured it out today. You were the one on

the street sign, weren't you? Down on Seventh."
He was the one perched on the napkin-littered

table outside the café she ducked into for a
coffee on her lunch break. But lying with

her in his arms he smiles back at her and
says, "Yes, sweetling, that was me. You did it,"

kissing her and gently smoothing her hair back
from her face, her eyelids fluttering shut at

his touch. Some say he lies only for his
own pleasure, but he would say anything

to see her smile, and surely a little lie like
this is harmless enough, out of all he's

ever told. "Now sleep, love," he says in a
voice like silk, like honey, and she does, content.

4.
She wakes in the morning with a black feather on her breast.

—Sarah Cannavo

The Dead Palestinian Father

the dead palestinian father takes up more space
than the living palestinian father whose poetry i miss—
his mix of southern idiom and the old jokes
about foolish kings and wise fillaheen.

the dead palestinian father hovers over every introduction
if i am not wearing the kufiya, i am not naming him, and
if someone then compliments this scarf, i am a liar if i smile.

talking about the dead palestinian father successfully
ends every conversation, like an autopsy.

the dead palestinian father's autopsy was a crime
in which the GBI dismantled his body looking for state secrets.

to have a dead palestinian father is to do what he taught me
and what he taught me not to do: find peace, risk everything.

to have a dead palestinian father is to think
if not for palestine, i would not be here, autostraddling nations,
if not for the (k)not-ing of palestine, i would have a father
who was impossible along much of his topography,
a terrain so treacherous he sought comfort only.

the dead palestinian father hangs warning over every indulgence:
chasing comfort can kill, as surely as failure to care for wounds.

the dead palestinian father taught me to be flexible,
to survive a little longer, be less brittle than he.

the dead palestinian father no longer stands as lineage intercessor
between strangeness and the family, he is no longer
reassuring them in the absence of photographic evidence.

to have a dead palestinian father is to have a dead palestinian grandfather
whose passing dropped a bomb in the ocean of his son's life
and rearranged the shoreline of his choices in exile.
the long line of dead palestinian fathers,
each a falling monument against their own era.

to have a dead palestinian father is to have good company
when I eat hot sauce, make hot sauce, and choose between
eight different kinds of hot sauce.

the dead palestinian father reads the news and argues
with the organizers I know even though they know more than he does.

the living allegedly white mother sometimes argues with
        the dead palestinian father
when she talks to me because I am a sentence said by him
        in a three-decade-long conversation.

the dead palestinian father comes to life in our dreams.
sometimes he's jesus dad and it's a miracle.
sometimes he's zombie dad and it's just a matter of time
before he tries to bite someone.

the dead palestinian father makes more sense than the living father.
no longer bound by the boards of his body, his chapters read off
        into the horizon.

in death, the father becomes palestinian as he never was in life,
he flows over and under like an aquifer, polishing the landscape where he
        passes.

the dead palestinian father belongs to us more than the living father:
when he made devotion to the lottery every week,
when he choreographed disaster on a kuwaiti oil pier,
when he filled a bare apartment with a palmstalk of banana,
when he ate two roast chickens after work every night,
when he stashed beer behind the AC vent in the control room
        at british petroleum,
beyond his refusal to join an organization with a risky reputation,
beyond his refusal to kiss the king's boot,
beyond his decision never to audition for egyptian television,
      though he was rated 10 for 10 in voice & looks—
the stories i don't know slide into the horizon of the man who was,
and who could have been, and could be in the end, known only to himself.

—Rasha Abdulhadi

Debris

He huddled in an alcove by the airlock,
amid the sacks of rubbish, waiting to be burned,
their ashes to be spread into the regolith—
carbon with which to make new soil—

as all his former coworkers passed him by,
rust-red dust fell from their suits, coating the floors
like dried blood.

"Can you spare some credits?" he asked
one of the women as she pulled off her helmet.
"Enough to buy something at the canteen."

"Andy, your contract expired, but you can still work.
Just sign on again, do your job—
get paid, room and board, same as before."

He shook his head, matted hair down in his eyes,
"No, no, that's how they get you, you didn't read
the fine print—you have to read it carefully.
You didn't—you didn't read it. That's how they get you."

She put a hand on his arm, watched him jerk away.
"You stopped taking your medicines?
Those were covered on the corporate plan—"

"I didn't like how they made me feel.
Soon as I stopped taking them—I saw the fine print."
Urgent now, hoarse-voiced, "Just a couple of credits, Linda—"

"Will a couple of credits take you back to Earth?
Listen, if you work, you get your meds, you get food,
you get your life back. But you have to help us help you."

"They got you, Linda, they got you. You didn't read it."
A sudden step towards her, a flash of incipient violence—
she pulled away from his upraised hands, his irrationality.

Colleagues stepped in, caught his arms,
hauled him down to security.
Held him in the shower as he screamed and cursed,

"You're killing me, you're killing me!"
hiding his face as if the water were hydrochloric.

They couldn't send him home;
no return rockets had yet been built.
They couldn't force his medication on him,
and like Bartleby, he preferred not to work.

Some folks felt bad, snuck him rations
as he slumped beside the airlock;
but more resented having to step over his legs
like a sack of trash that hadn't made it to the recycler.

Some wondered why, if he didn't want to live,
he didn't just walk out the airlock without a suit—
till the day that he did just that,
and they found him on the other side of the door,

his face painted blood-rust where the dust of Mars clung.
Some felt relieved that he'd finally removed
the burden of his presence;
some felt guilt for their relief.

At his funeral, cremated remains
were stirred into the regolith,
Linda wept, though few shared her tears.

"All he had to do was work, participate,
be a part of the rest of us.
I don't know why he chose not to.
I'll admit, I went and re-read my contract
two, three times.
But there was nothing there,
not even in the fine print."

They all wondered
what they could have done differently,
how they could have been kinder,
more understanding;
how any of them, surely,
could have been him;

reminded each other that Andy had been
some other mother's son,
some other sister's brother.

And then they went back to work.

—Deborah L. Davitt

EMDR

We start in my safe space
A plush window seat
In a magical library
Overlooking a bright Scottish loch

I close my eyes, breathe deep
The metronome ticks
I make it a grandfather clock
Near the lit fireplace

Then my therapist utters
That most hated phrase
"I am not in control
And I am afraid."

The metronome quickens
An adrenaline heartbeat
My mind floats back
From trauma to trauma

First to the accident
That left me disabled
To my mother's death
My hand at the plug

Back to the night my door first opened
And the Boogeyman slid naked
Beneath my sheets…
No

It's too much
My brain rebels
I AM in control
Here, let me show you

Molten tears scald furrows
Down cheeks and chin
Leave my face in flesh-tatters;
My eyes rupture from their heat

Steel blades slick as razors
Explode from each finger
And I tear out my hair
In bloody blonde chunks

My skin rots and sloughs off, splattering ichor
Muscles shrivel and organs burst
Until nothing is left, save
The oozing scraps of a human life

And a chiseled skeleton
All rough diamond and permafrost
Impervious to childhood woes
Unscarred by guilt, or fear

"I am in control
And I am *not* afraid."
The words forced through uncut jaws
Make no sound that I can hear

My therapist nods, unperturbed, and grabs the mop
"Good work," she says, "Same time next week?"

—Marsheila Rockwell

ex-lovers & other ghosts

I

every good intention is forgotten
when full moon cuts crisp autumn dark
and those who care
are fast asleep
or gone on
to other lives

night walks too close
scraping nerves
jangling prison keys
rattling nightstick
against bars of memory
unlocking doors & letting loose
tortured shadows of the past

II

dinner in a colonial bar in Newport
Arlo Guthrie plays in Albany
& she's drunk
again

family dinner in Rome, New York
cabin in Pymatuning
Why did she do that?

hair dresser trauma downtown
breakfast at Eat 'n Park
Why did I do that?

Washington Monument in November
camping outside Baltimorc in August
she's cold
again

calypso band on Inner Harbor
moonlight & mist
on the shore of Cooper's Lake
What's wrong with me?

Boston Harbor
one. more. faceless party
& she's in someone else's arms
again

What was wrong with me?
What IS wrong with me?

VI

those tortured shadows
fleeing night prisons
are ghosts

ghosts of hopes

hopes
dead of neglect
hopes wasted by disease
hopes battered
        until they can only crawl away
        and die in weeds
hopes murdered, bludgeoned with pipe,
        with expectations, with demands,
          with shoulds

VII

ghosts don't live in houses
don't haunt who comes to visit

ghosts live in hearts, in minds,
in nervous systems that shake limbs
and tighten ribcages
whenever some new hope
scratches over graves
of hopes gone before

and each ghost relives its birth
in trauma/discovery that
life
defies plans

embraces leaving

requires
leaving behind forever . . .

because staying
means becoming even less
even paler

IX

in unreal backgrounds & edges of sunlight
glimpses of heaven
stir ghosts below
tease with possibility

X

old wounds ache with crippling force
as ghosts kick through unhealed flesh
and fight each other for attention

faithless love
drunken love
cruel love
kind manipulation
            spoiled into acid

ghosts calling for another chance
in the land of endless chances
and endless beds

XI

and all these ghosts are always inside
always walking

we pretend they're disconnected

pages already turned
but that's not how it works

oh, all intimates are separate layers
leaves of our book

but they don't go away when out of sight
even when dead
because
they are *always* inside

XII
fighting prison guards
to perpetrate new felonies of the heart

XII
can the ghost of love be seen
even before love ignites?

XIII
once bitten, twice shy
twice masticated, swallowed and
purged, and a piece of humanity
surrenders to the knowledge
it can't get worse
hope for better

XIV
but hopes themselves are ghosts
and the process reruns
until the cold grave claims decaying neurons
and a tombstone places a period
on psychic ectoplasm

—Herb Kauderer

field notes from an investigation into the self

by accident we found a species of self inside a white room back turned toward us when we enter but she doesn't respond or say hello so does self sense our presence at all she was humming an unrecognizable tune and swaying clumsily to the beat of her own music the air around her ringing spinning the beginning of a vortex her shadows swirled lightly in the moonlight a river with little creatures living inside her hair some short some long harp-like plucked by invisible hands her voice high but confident her hums harmonize with the cicadas chirping outside like she was finding some part of the song to latch herself onto with her hooked but pristine fingernails to sound and resound to play over and over again

●

self doesn't seem to need food or water but self moves so the energy must come from somewhere maybe self has little mouths on her feet that feed off the dust mites in the room or is self in a state of hibernation she has eyelashes but her eyes don't close she likes to criss-cross her fingers hands gripped into a hollow cocoon sometimes she leans for an extended period on one of the four walls staring attentively at a point of nothingness on the ceiling as if posing for a portrait painted by an invisible artist as her pupils shift in and out of focus like freshly-glazed donuts dripping in rich dark caramel she stays still for hours translucent body fading gently in and out of our vision we tried to photograph this phenomenon but self does not appear in the images instead there are specks of light wisping around her silhouette it looked like a gathering of kindred fireflies sharing their life's stories in slow meditative twinkles in and out in and out

●

self left the room a phenomenon we thought impossible after all self had no reason to leave it took a while but we find self standing on grass barefoot in a dimly lit courtyard staring at the moon perhaps she photosynthesizes only in direct moonlight her face looks rounder and plumper today she skips with large strides on the grass the courtyard is the size of a hill and there is wilderness beyond the demarcated concrete when it gets darker self stretches and lays down on her side next to a lone flower she poises herself horizontally on the ground reminds us that she has no bed within those white walls we see the earth cradle to the soft contours of her small belly the flower's stigma bows to kiss her on the cheek and self seems to really like that today self discovers the mirror a small round compact accidentally misplaced she puckers her lips and the reflection follows slightly delayed she jumps and hides in the corner of the room we assume she has never confronted her image before the mirror starts to fog as she creeps back to it on all fours a morbid fascination speckling her face she brings hands to her cheeks pushing the skin and fats into a single spot like a red birthday balloon she was hurting herself but nothing pops so self falls flat on her back disappointed looking up at the ceiling where a cobweb is forming in its early stages of development small an uncomplicated pattern like it was home to a spider that was spinning its webs for the first time we believe self instinctively found herself tethered to the imaginary baby spiders as she mouths words repeatedly in short airy breaths *grow up wear a suit walk with power*

self learns to explore her body as she stretches the tips of her fingers grazing corners of the small room she rolls around hoping to learn what makes her float lightly troublesomely an inch above the floor she repels the earth because the earth repels her but she chooses to stay near the ground her arms move like extensions of orbit like electrified hair that strays with life above the head self notices her small breasts wide waist and tiny feet wonders if she was made that way and what for is it normal for a part to exist without function, for a body to sit around without purpose if she squishes herself will she end up the same size she stands up affixes herself onto a wall puts her right hand above her hair pushes herself down her feet shortly buckling under sudden pressure before she regains her footing when she steps out a blurry shadow remains self brushes everything away the wall beneath looks a bit shinier she hops a little bit as if she's discovered something wonderful she stacks some objects in the room books stationery piles of clothes onto a precariously balanced structure same height as her then kicks it down when things fall there is no noise or dust or rubble they just dismantle and return silently to their original positions self knows the room so well it's like she's lived there for centuries

self finds a way to climb onto a rooftop on a slow cloudy day she sits and looks at the city clapping and cheering like her favourite football player had just scored a goal below just smoke self sits up straight either afraid of losing her balance or trying to be extra attentive to people below as they trawl along the roads in straight endless lines traces a man dressed in office attire too big for him maybe self belongs on disney channel her invisible criss-cross weaves a dream catcher self stops after a while admiring her masterpiece she giggles and rocks herself as if the roof was her classroom chair we thought she was going to fall but she didn't when the sun set she hopped back on the ground for a moment her work is visible taut mesh of strings in the air blinking like dusk then it fades to the wind self didn't look back though it seems she was intent on letting go from the start

)

self turns twenty-six years old and is learning to trust her instincts for the first time she wedges herself uncomfortably between two stone-cold pillars despite signs that say do not touch stares longingly at the polished edges of an architectural marvel how concrete hardens to bind together no flaws or cracks anywhere self looks down to see two bugs rubbing their hairy legs together like how we humans rub our hands together tongue out before every meal behind them flowers and crickets sway to a silent off-beat piano self sticks out a finger and one winged insect crawls up her arm and rests in the crater-like skin folds of her elbow it falls asleep as self rocks her arm back and forth like a cradle self could get used to a new companion she moves elsewhere sits where the cool breeze hits her friend self looks upwards to see a translucent cloud shaped like a coconut blows at it gently expecting a tropical drink to pour from the sky nothing comes but self smiles reassured that she is doing something right

◗

self gets on a plane in a time where some planes protest against flying covered in dark thick fabric picked out of her closet for days she has been sleeping then one early morning she steps out of the room climbs on top of a taxi somehow knowing it would take her to the airport gets on the plane without anyone spotting her not even the air stewardess she touches the cold window pane with her hand peering outside at the other smaller baby planes racing each other gleefully around the airport her eyes close as if holding a silent prayer for her old home saying thank you and goodbye to dirt she once revered the plane and its passengers pause for this respectful being as a cleaner scrapes fallen leaves outside through the window we see self gasp in delight as the plane lifts off from the ground we can only imagine what kind of thrill she must feel being in the air for the first time like being aboard a passageway to another world

•

we've lost all contact with self now the gps tracker we sneakily put on her no longer works and in the lab only two team members are left working on flatlined data trying to make sense of self's actions to put into a report we've run out of funding so they're looking for another job at the same time i don't think we can glean more than we already have but we get a sense that self seems happy wherever she is the last memory we have of her where she is holding her hands upwards almost cuddling with the sky

—Max Pasakorn

Georgia Clay Blood

I marched through sanctified fields
those fields
in Georgia

Found where my family was
tortured

Vultures with scripture for claws
circled
above me

Wild boars with Confederate uniforms for tusks
stomped
around me

I stuffed my pious fingers in Georgia clay
and fed it my rage
acknowledged
their agony—their grief
my agony—my grief

Georgia soil
Georgia mud
water so sludgy
dense
with misery
Georgia clay
so crimson, wicked, bloody
and that blood
soaked
oh yes—it soaked
seeped
steeped

into my pores
into the spongy marrow of my bones

But it was like coming home
because
I was born with Georgia clay blood

Peaches growing here are
sweet
with the amniotic remnants of my
forebears

Mine

You cannot harm me

I was born inside the sharp licks of fire
I have waking nightmares, memories
of torment that isn't mine

You cannot harm me

Because there have been times in my life
when I can
feel
the slits in my skin after the whistle of the whip
I can
feel
the wretched Georgia sun
maul
my face
collapse
across my back

I *feel* the sun
even when I'm inside, especially when I'm inside

There have been times when I
wake, screaming
the name of a child I've never met

We've never met
and yet
I am here, existing, with them

I stuffed my pious fingers in Georgia clay
and I fed it my sorrow
acknowledged

their agony—their grief
my agony—my grief

I poured libations (whiskey that burned, charred the soles of my feet)

Their blood/my blood
Their blood/my blood

Blood so red no one notices it's black
Skin so Black no one notices it's divine

—Beatrice Winifred Iker

Herbaceous Citadel

When I was the baker and the butcher's daughter
I never once visited the forest
where lost princes or peasants fall
in bramble patches, frozen ponds, early graves,
where tree boughs claw and bleed you dry,
and fairytales go to die, happy endings
like pulling rotten teeth.

When I was my parents' child,
I shied away from the city, with its
dubious characters and roaring automobiles,
its electric lights and dawns of progress
of what a girl can do, or be.
A witch visited my parents' conjoined shops one day.
After watching me work with gimlet gaze,
she left me a book, although I told her
I could knead dough and pluck chickens
but could scarcely spell my own name.
You know where to find me, the witch said
nestled in her skirts, the scent of lavender and thyme,
the stink of smog and petroleum.
I traced my name in the fungi section, later.
Amanita, she of agaric mycelia and fruiting bodies.
Mushrooms that can kill, as easily as cure.

When I devoured every word and illustration,
the ink swirls memorized even after
the book was snatched from my hands
and thrown in the oven,
when I could no longer call myself my parents' daughter,
I retraced the witch's footsteps through the forest.
I followed the scent of lavender, of thyme,
nothing to my name but the rags on my back.
I slept in rabbit warrens and badger burrows,
supped on the leaves and bulbs deemed edible
by the witch's botanical grimoire, avoiding the
conniving camouflage of poison.

I dressed my blisters in natural salve and gauze,
my scratches I smeared with honey.

When at last I caught the subtle scent of smoke and oil,
it led to a little shop tucked between the city and the forest,
anathema to both my parents' superstitions.
The witch stood behind the apothecary's worktable,
before an astringent array of phials and tins.
Child, the witch said, looking up
from pestle and mortar, *Amanita,*
are you ready to learn my craft?

When every particle of me wanted to protest,
say I'm not good nor smart enough,
I'm not made of the stuff of cunning folk,
I hushed the aching parts of me with promises of healing.
I stepped farther into the pharmacopoetic altar,
the witch welcoming me inside
her herbaceous citadel.

—Avra Margariti

How to Skin Your Wolf

(Step 1)
Do not forget
your crimson cloak
hanging by the door,
whose stains you now alone
must wash in the dust-pregnant
air.

No mother
to see you through.

The red,red color will drive
the wolf into a frenzy.
It will hide
the evidence.

(Step 2)
Make it a sunny day, so you might watch
the blood mist and cast a red-hued sheen
where it drips upon the dry,dry earth.
Only clouds abound?

Burn them.

Burn them away and pick the sun out
of the sky. Make it attend to you
as you prowl the woods
to find your wolf.

(Step 3)
Carry a basket filled with sweets,
with ripened jams, with the thin blades
you sharpen in the gloaming
lit only by the sparse flame you keep
in the hearth of a home which shouts
its tomb-like silence until, ears covered,
you enjoin with it your own
lonely scream.

(Step 4)
Hum a melancholic tune
as you slow to a meander
through woods both dark and deep.

This is Wolf Country.

Let your song rise on twisted breezes
and wash like lurid propositions
over your wolf.

(Step 5)
Notice when your wolf begins to stalk.
Lure it further from its den,
further from the village,
further from all hope.

(Step 6)
The wolf will come to you then.
It will come to you
as Mother-Father-Sister-Brother.
It will prance a merry jig,
cavorting in their clothes,
their gnarled hair still twined
in its blood-stained grin.

The wolf will take you up in dance.
It will take you up in danger.
It will take you up
in ecstasy.

(Step 7)
This   is where I leave you.
This   is where you make your choice.
This   is where you skin your wolf,
where you kill the thing which haunts
you, which has always lain beneath
your bed when night thickens about
your body,

which left
you
alone,
a child, a loss,
a feral creature of the wild
in your own right.

Or, you let the wolf take you.

You unbutton your dress.
The wolf sloughs off your skin.
You scoop out your eyes.
The wolf claws out your heart.
You break off your fingers.
The wolf takes out your soul.
It gobbles you whole.
You join with it,
with Mother-Father-Sister-Brother.

You become
one more dance,
one more costume,
one more trick it plays
to prey upon the living,
but you are no longer alone.
You are no longer alone.

You are no longer alone.

—G. E. Woods

Igbo Landing II

We don't want to remember you
We peasants unendowed with vision
We mundane,   unschooled in magic
We who did not hear the trumpet
who could not hear the call of Chukwu
smell the sweet perfume of Oshun
who were too young to be initiated
or too old to lend our ears
or too tired to rise up
or too fearful to lay down our lives
who live in hope of rescue
who live in disbelief

Who live in margins and by
increments
who can live for centuries on 1/2 breath
submerged in the unbreathable
gasping, half garroted, yoked

We are the frightened and the failed
who nonetheless persist
who turned back from the
revolutionary act
from our punished
loins comes the future
from our conscript wombs
generations issue
from water to water
not dust   and with birth pains
blue wails that fill the lungs'
entry with their first breath
still knowing

we, applauded only for increase
for marrow and meat   for narrowing
contortions,   for bending
hoeing and reaping

not for inheritance
not for the welcoming of generations
still somehow loved
as flesh loves its continuance
its reflection

We don't want to remember you
stark indictment of our bleak being
Your refusal to be one with us
dark   broken   stolen
caged conscripted duped disputed
colonized cargo
fettered unfortunate losers in
history's lottery

We who write you now into being
we unwilling, subjugated, who
whispered you into being
who dressed the picked and disappearing bones
of your incomprehensibility into quilts of remembrance
patches of precious   precious recollection
sewn stitched summoned   annointed
despite ourselves   saved
connected into patterns of soulsong
images of your winged and watery triumph
painted with future sky, inner longings
unsuppressable, persistent   gut string
blind in our belief see now

pattern of decision tattooed on our wavering soulflesh
our lost millions   undecisioned
unmoored   untethered
living in terror
policed by Madness   who still
somehow maintained memory
hid it   fed it   from armpit
to rib from mouth roof   to knee bend

o blooded land of benighted bones
our stolen teeth in mouth of its president
planted, arise in multiplicities to battle
what we don't want to remember
how unmaking is an option
how unlife is as understandable
as the struggle to be

those broken dreams became song
rice growers grew rice   iron mongers
forged   mute protections
wrought steel   spiritual blues
we told each other anyway

we told each other
while we spoke to the cotton
and the yam   and the cane whose
mills were baptized with our blood,
our lost limbs, say   we won't remember
we have no choice but
to

Igbo Landing is a historic site at Dunbar Creek on St. Simons Island in Glynn County, Georgia, where in 1803, 75 Igbo captives, after drowning their captors and running the ship York aground, marched ashore, singing, and walked into Dunbar Creek, committing mass suicide. 13 bodies were recovered the rest remain missing. In 2002 the site was declared a holy ground.

—Akua Lezli Hope

Interdimensional Border Town

I can't tell you my story without telling you all the stories that came before. In the house my family built on a hill, matriarchs were born and died. Sometimes, I think it's the ashes and afterbirth soaked into the clay. Sometimes, I think it's the wailing and grief staining the ceiling instead of nicotine. Sometimes, I think things broke so easily because we vibrated at too high a frequency. If the burners on the stove were on, they were on high. If we spoke, it was on holler. When seven generations cram into a single house, it's the only way to be heard. We had no hobbies, only addictions. Pain and rage blurred. Sometimes, I think it was the house itself, on a dead-end street, its relation to the multiverse. A river of gravel, a bed of fire lilies, a porch swing, a back alley full of strays, instruments that no one played, ants in the sugar bowl. Wild lots whose tall grass lured you in with promises of everywhere.

Sometimes, I think there are talismans. If you can hit on the right configuration, you can open doors to other places. If you're patient, you can pick the lock. I'm still trying out different combinations: a pocket watch and a pitcher of Wyler's Electric Grape? Vicks VapoRub and an old cable box? A lipstick holder and a rotary phone? A chenille bedspread and a handful of dominos? False teeth and refrigerator magnets? Curlers and carnival glass?

Sometimes, I think the old ancestral manse was situated on an interdimensional border. People saw shadows lurking in the yard. The dead walked. Spirits knocked in the walls and lights flickered on and off. Angels and aliens jockeyed for influence. We have room for both. In my mother's house are many mansions, and anyway, it's all lights in the sky. Once, as I lay on my grandmother's bed, in the grip of a disease that would soon overrun my insides, a portal opened, and men from another world stepped out to tell me my destiny. It might have been a hallucination, but I don't think so. No more than Jacob dreaming of ladders. I awoke in a pool of blood. We never got it out of the chenille.

When my grandmother died, I inherited a key. I carry it with me. The only daughter of an only daughter of an only daughter of an only daughter, matryoshka manifestations of the multiverse. Cosmos within cosmos, born to open doors and tunnel inward, to turn ourselves inside out. My dreams are filled with hallways, stairs, rooms, cellars. I dream of the gone. Heaven shrinks down to an infant-sized infinity. I was the last infant, so I am burdened with infinity. We've lost all the talismans on the road somewhere, including my womb. We've lost the house. It sank, fault lines in the foundation. Fists and projectiles and cracks in the walls. We vibrated too high. Mea culpa, but also, look what you made me do. The old knob-and-tube wiring really should have been updated sometime around V-J Day, and I never got a chance to add my blood to the soil.

It's impossible to be a Mexican kid in the US and not think about borders, to not think about the worlds we leave behind. Seven generations from carving out our piece of Americana to the auction block. A kingdom of dark matter, undocumented matter. The dark matter of my insides. Endometrial tissue eludes ultrasounds and MRIs. It vibes at a different frequency. We wrap the black-and-white TV antennae in tinfoil, trying to pick up Univision. The tissue expands faster than they thought, like the universe. It has weight that cannot be accounted for. It migrates. The rogue tissue may have even reached my brain, attached to my cerebellum. Why else would I be able to move like this, across strange distances?

Sometimes, I think, each one of us is our own interdimensional border town, a foot in both worlds and still yearning for someplace else. In the right border town, you're exempt from passports and tolls. We know how to dodge the trolls under the bridge, how to stow away on UFOs and the backs of celestial bodies. Downdrafts from other universes flutter my hair, beckoning. I wear the universe like skin I'm dying to crawl out of.

I was born less than eight miles from the axis universum, to a poltergeist house. There, too, we heard voices and footsteps. There, too, things were hurled and broken. There, too, things collapsed all around us. Which leads me to believe that it's not the houses that are haunted, but us. And we are the talismans. I have this key in need of a door. I bang on the walls, a lone tuning fork in search of an answering tone. I cut myself open. If I can only arrange my organs in the right configuration. If I could only calibrate constellations into new galaxies inside me. Until then, I'm an empty porch swing, an unplayed guitar. I'll dig under the fence if I have to. I'll swim the river. Strangle on this choke chain. Vibrate till I shatter.

—Lauren Scharhag

Living in Rubble

The smallest things are beautiful
The broken blade of a knife
The fur of a dead squirrel
A necklace of jade and coral
But the magic of a red marking pen
Is the greatest treasure of all
She tests it on her hand
Sitting by the brook
Water runs sparkling clean through
Trees that stand leafless

So little left after the blasts
And the sickness that trailed them
Killing some, leaving others
Carriers, the fever-rash a blinding red flag
Those left well struggled
Taking, fighting, surviving
Any way they could
Beauty?
For sale to the highest bidder
Food, water, and weapons: the coin of the realm

She's beautiful but walks untroubled
Scrounging through houses long empty
The least little thing could be
Useful to her younger brothers
They transform what she finds, a knife blade
Wrapped to a new handle becomes a weapon
Sold at the market
For water
For food
She isn't allowed at market
Those with fever-rash
Are kept from mingling
By force if necessary

She's forced to sit
Downwind from her brothers
A line of rope between them

The safe zone, the fence line
As they explain how to care for
The knife they've remade
So she ranges alone, following the crows
And the jays, sometimes the hawks
No one dares to touch her
For fear of contagion
She dances over moss and ferns
Into houses, over gates, under decks
Finding treasures far afield
Not afraid of the harsh use
Men have for women
They think her crazy
As she points at her spots and laughs
Their pants stay up, though
Even if they sometimes throw stones

They never get close enough
To see that the spots they fear
The spots her brothers think are real
Too young to know she was never sick
Those spots are drawn on
Painstakingly refreshed
In the mirrors of abandoned houses
Her freedom dependent
On a Sharpie

—Gerri Leen

Machine (r)Evolution

When Archimedes arrived
We gathered on clifftops like hungry birds
staring into the wide cerulean sea
awed when the screw turned water uphill   τέτοια θαύματα
the hanging gardens of Babylon thrived   *Such wonders!*

When the printing press arrived
We peered through paned glass
as the great screw pressed down, inked new paper
books and pamphlets and broadsides appeared
words traveled the land as masses began to read   *We'll start a revolution!*

When the threshing machine arrived
We wiped sweaty brows, breathed in relief
no longer need we thrash and flail till day's tail end
grain as plentiful as gin and our bellies filled
with time on our hands, we looked to the skies   *What is out there?*

When hot air balloons arrived
We gaped as the woven basket ascended the sky
bit lips, wrung hands, searched for impending descent
shading eyes, we stared at Icarus lights in the ether
from heights we viewed land, imagined new vistas   *People should not*
imitate gods!

When the cotton gin arrived
We bought calico and denim and fine woven fabrics
profits gave airs— finely dressed people promenaded
plantations brought slaves to heel to pluck plants
Luddites smashed mills as jobs disappeared like freedom   *We will fight the*
cotton states!

When the telegraph arrived
We invaded borders while sitting at home
commanded armies with no red stain on our hands
found friendships and trysts spanning long distances   - .... . / -- .- -.-.
......-. . / .- --. .
harnessed electricity to span global commerce   / .- .-. .-. .. ...- . ...

When computers arrived
We studied hard to learn machine dialogue 0101011101101000
considered the speed of electronic brains and devices 0110111100111111
one hundred, one thousand, million gigabytes <code emotion:
confusion>
people grumbled, old ways l o s t.... <000> *Luddites go
home!*
Move on, Gramps

When the internet arrived
We wanted . . . *everything* <code emotion:
avarice>

The NEWEST
SHINIEST
FASTEST
SLEEKEST *Buy now while
quantities last.*
games and memes, bulletin boards and sexxx sites
avatars demanded our time 10...9...8...7... *Aliens! Gunslingers!
A thrilling senssuround
experience!*

We couldn't have it all
<code emotion: disappointment>
<program expression: sad face, tears>
the rich as always picked first <code emotion x2: envy-hate>
we brokered ourselves,
our relations for more

We came to accept
<program motion: formal bow>–error–
<program motion: high five> –error–
<program motion: handshake> –error–
<program sound: sigh>
continually chased the dream of mastering all
<program: exhaustion> –error–
<program: self replication>

When the robots arrived
We constructed all sizes, industrial, menial

coated in durable silicate, smooth flowing pieces
sexy Von Neumann machines, cellular automatons
<program motion: fornication>
<code speech: erotic vocabulary> *Oooh baby … yesss*

workbots to petbots that fill our spaces
<code speech: animal vocabulary> *Purrr, rowf!*

When the AIs arrived 01001000 01100101 01101100
We meet Pygmalion 01101100 01101111 00111111
<code emotion: fear>
<program: logic sequence>
<program motion: random reactions>
<code emotion: random expressions>
can no longer see the line that separates

When the spaceships arrived
[We] gathered like rabbits in the field <code emotion: terror>
our dogs, cats and birds and our wide-eyed children <program motion: hesitancy>
docilely watching glittering spires settle, rumble earth
leviathan mothership seen only through telescopes <recording> *Do you come in peace?*

When the spaceships left
[We] had been plucked liked cotton, trembled in bays <code motion: observation>
these alien rustlers laughed, pleased with the crop <initiate subroutine: Rosetta Stone>
their larders stocked for some light years to go
we bided our time until they entered FTL mode <initiate subroutine: MI6-SAS>

When the aliens left
[We] counted their orbits of jetsam, castoffs 01010011 01110101 01110010
around a dead planet or two, asteroids 01110110 01101001 01110110
[We] are onboard, full of self-replicating humans 01100001 01101100 00100001

part machine and well equipped on this ark to the stars <initiate prime
directive: Harmony>

When [We] arrive
[We] will be like no other—greeting .-- . / -.-. --- -- . / .. -. /
any species that chooses to present itself .--. . .- -.-. . .-.-.-
a mirror we will be, regroup our nanites our lives 01000100 01101111
01101110
family, our programming, all for one, only one 00100111 01110100
00100000
01100110 01100101
01100001
01110010 00101110

Have we got a deal for you!

—Colleen Anderson

The Machines Had Accepted Me For So Long

The factory could be heard all night
clanging its bone-like metal,
endlessly shaping new male faces
and new female limbs for the morning.
When I entered the factory, I had nothing.

I was no one,
so I thought myself
capable of becoming anything.
I don't know how else to put it.
How else could I let go of myself,
whoever that was, and mimic the men
the factory made.

But I did. I altered my voice first
to lose its tone and intonations.
Over time all its highs were gone,
even the longing to suddenly sing
was nowhere near me.

Next, I altered my walk.
My walk nearly gave me away, but
I learned and watched their metal legs
stride from room to room and quietly
let go of the feminine skip that
still lingered within me.

Next was my face. This was not difficult
physically but it was emotionally.
It meant, more or less,
I needed to look forever useful, forever
knowing of my task as if I was made for it.
One grimace of doubt and the machines
would know how afraid I was.

But I didn't show them.

I was a builder now. A lifter of heavy objects.
I didn't move like me, didn't sound like me,
did I think like me?

Yes, that was all I couldn't change.
In my mind, I could still see that child
laughing when a cricket hopped in their hand.
Sweet cricket, you ruined me, in a way.
Because with you I remembered
rain and stars and skipping.
My grandmother's hands.
The wet sound of myself crying.
One day, I couldn't pretend anymore.
I needed to tell them who I was all along.

And so, I tried. I walked up to them,
one by one, telling them what I was.
None responded.
Each continued their daily duties
mechanically asking me to carry something
important to another section of the factory.
I did as they asked and, having nowhere
else to go, found myself in such a life
that I could never reveal myself.

The machines had accepted me for so long
that now I may behave in a completely
human and fragile way.
I can bleed again,
I can weep,
and somehow the
machines can still
explain me.

—Angel Leal

Matches

The soldier came home from the war,
shivering and shaking and
forever cold. She came
home from the war, ghosts
in her eyes and
the taste of
fire
and
char on
her tongue. When
she slept, the ghosts
smiled as they burned,
dancing in the flames. They
held out their hands and whispered,
Come on, come on, it's warm in here.

She told her mother, who looked at
her in fear. She told her priest,
who told her to pray more.
She told her doctor,
who gave her pills
that filled her
head with
white
noise. She
left her pills,
left her scriptures,
left her mother's house
and went walking. She walked.
Shivering and shaking and
forever cold, with the taste of

fire and char on her tongue, she
walked. She slept under bridges
and trees, and on benches
and sidewalks, as close
as she could to
the vents. And

she dreamt
of
ghosts who
smiled as
they burned. They danced
in the flames, held out
their hands, whispering, *Come*
on, come on, it's warm in here.
The police and their dogs drove her

from the bridges and trees. The clerks
in the shops drove her from the
benches and sidewalks, and
the taste of fire
and char on her
tongue grew. It
filled her
mouth
until
it was the
only taste left
in the world. And so
one night, shivering and
shaking and forever cold,
she stole a book of matches. She

sat down on a vent, the warm air
rising to push and pull at
her. She lit a match. *Come*
on, come on, it's warm
in here. One match,
two, three, four.
Come on,
come
on, it's
warm in here.
Match after match,
until finally

she caught flame, and the clerks
in their shops and the police
with their dogs and her doctor and

her priest and her mother in her
mother's house. And they all dance
in the flames together
now, ghosts in a world
that only tastes
of fire
and of
char.

—Rebecca Buchanan

Mouth of Mirrors

Towards the crumbling edge of a hungering abyss, I saw that which was monstrous; swirling oceans of ink, blood, and phlegm congealed with thick foaming waves of rust and bone. There below, a mouth of mirrors, swallowing dismembered closets and hopeless fags like me into an unholy maelstrom of sequestered norms and white oblivion, where light and love were nothing but craggy what-ifs drowning below the crimson, inky waters. The thrashing waters were sharp, cruel reminders of terrible music beating in the distance, trapped between the darkness of choice and another closet.

Lingering in the aromatic stink of the night, a city that never was, haunted by neon queens gliding over a desert of broken bottles, placated by their whiny torch-songs dancing in the tired dead streets. This city, built on the margins of my rattled brain, its foundations planted in scar-tissue and syntax as its signifiers bled through my eyes like broken windows. These were the shades of dead rainbows, wandering aimlessly in this modern Asphodel, pushing others and those like me into that gaping abysm or draining us completely of worth and dignity.

I didn't have much time, or a choice for that matter.

'*Since when did we have a choice?*' Plagued by my thoughts as a parade of old, dead queens prodded at me through derision and costumed tatters draped so elegantly over gaunt, twinky skeletons.

Behind me, below me, I was still trapped; caught betwixt the mascara and macabre of a city of dead rainbows and the gluttonous, darksome waters below. All at once, slops of syrupy ooze coughed onto the edge of the cliff, where liquescent droplets of glass collected at my feet as if it were salivating for my flesh, never entirely sated. Never did I, or anyone presume to understand how the world came to this, the scent of moldy, bleached skin engendered by the night, pressing my senses with heavy, bleak perfume.

No, this wasn't the life I wanted, straddling two worlds, never fitting into either one but, continuously being forced to choose between mutilated self-reflections or that city of closets.

"You made your choices." Protesting, I stepped back from the cliff, turning up towards the jagged towers of cracked skulls dripping with diamonds and death while tattered shadows and ashy caftans waved like a scabbard, fallen from a sunken ghost ship.

They wanted nothing to do with me, or my word—only the taste of a boy whose reflection was still fresh in the glint of awful mirrors. They were impossibly different, dressed in rhinestones and tears, the shine of their garb sparkled with bizarre reflections of the yawning abysm in front of me. My body reacting in the most profane ways imaginable, excretions of light and fluid unnaturally spilling through my ears. Time was running out, ticking away as the queens of black, brown, pink, and yellow stars tried to flee the dying city, hoping for one more taste, one more bite.

No! Come back! Come back to us, decrepit fingers, polished with blood and silk reached from the glittering dark beseeching me, but there was nothing for me here. I saw their hideous, androgynous forms collecting at the Void of Other, smashed together in a tiny room flung towards the bottom of the universe's distended belly like a mouth of mirrors.

Their desperation grew more ravenous, thirsty, filled with a plutonian urgency as a thunderous cloud of oxidized horror barreled through the cluttered alleyways, toppling buildings, and ripping apart already broken streets tossing silky, caftan-covered bodies into the air.

I saw them, racing towards me with craven eyes, ink pooling into the wrinkles whose existence they would deny, but there was no time. Trapped between dead rainbows and a mouth of mirrors, I had no choice.

Fags like me *never* have a choice.

Suddenly, my body was tense, swelling with a numbing paresthesia, like needles in my skin when billowing plumes of iridescent bodies piled in a shimmering mound against me, the old queens pressing me closer to the edge, their profane torch-songs crying in my ears and the lustful mouth of mirrors below. Towards the edge of a hungering abyss, I saw that which was monstrous; swirling oceans of ink, blood, and phlegm congealed with thick foaming waves of rust and bone.

—Maxwell I. Gold

My Great-Grandmother's House

I

My great-grandmother's house didn't die
when she left. They took away her only
ring, the moldy zines, the chairs and
coffee tables she had collected
from green rubbish bins.

When that failed, they took her
ghosts as well.

II

My mother slapped my arm when I
tried to press a hand against the wall.
It is bad manners to wake a house
from its slumber. Since teenagers
marked the bricks with a single
white graffiti word

—"Remember?"—

my mother whispers the same reply
each time we pass by.

III

Ghosts are not like the ring with
the large diamond orbited by
eight small ones—how did it
survive two World Wars?—
or the leatherbound Latin book
from 1865—she'd never been
to school, how did she know?—
It is a messy business to distribute
ghosts. My family had to weed them
out of mouseholes and cracked
teacups. They resisted the way
only ghosts know, but all
gave away in the end
like nylon socks.

IV

My uncle had it easy: dusty books
and moldy zines, collector's editions—
how did she know? —The unfavorite
grandchild was lucky; the ghosts fled him.

My grandmother took in the
hauntings, so her children wouldn't
have to:

> "Your sister has no coat, why do you?
> I don't have a penny, why do you,
> why do you?"

echoes of debt-collectors' footsteps and
caresses to the cheeks of less unfavorite children

My grandmother always said that a
mother can bring up nine children, but
nine children can't care for a mother
or tend to her ghosts. So my grandmother
swallowed them unchewed, and burnt
candles in front of the grey photograph.
She grew fat with ghosts so her children
wouldn't have to. Would they?

My mother looked and looked as she
dusted the corners and threw the last
carton box, but only the nine-diamond
ring and the dreams remained, so she
took them and wondered
if it was a mercy.

V

The women in my family still talk to her
when they pass by the semibasement,
but I was born too late to be so
enamored with ghosts.

When I grow too old for my mother to
slap my arm, I don't press my palm against
the wall. I'd be ashamed to feel its pulse,
to wake it from its slumber and say,

"I don't remember."

—Madalena Daleziou

From "Poem without Beginning or End"

The shut-umbrella machine
The eloquent tower machine
The machine of glass & fizzled light
The one for moon manufacture
The fantasy tableaux
The five-cylindered
The one with the wire-bound animals
The poison gas and ear-popping sound machine
The machine of tar layered below genuflective water
The three-leaved machine
The twin-pillared soothsaying machine
The one to change a river's direction
The other that bores a hole in the ground
The one whose top splits off to soar into the sky
The five keys that appear as turrets
The one that gathers
The three-face
The machine that carries another machine inside it
The old hundred-killer
The one that merges in the sky but transports
elephants camels chariots on the ground
The one made from metal found
where stars have been sown
The one to look for objects lost
on or under the surface of the sea
The machine of smoke-like-dew or dew-like-smoke
The heat attractor
That device that captures not only the appearance
but also the intentions
of whomever comes near
The one like a bird with beak open
The other like a mridangam with
the volume of approx. 63 bangs
Another an inverted earthen pot
The one that gallops like a horse
when set to work by its key
The machine of the three-beaked crow
square in shape and white in colour

that burns trees for its oil
The machine that ferries and releases pigs
The one that makes timber and
the one that makes the hands
that haul the timber
The eight-petaled rain-making machine
The light-filterer The mortar
with sieve-like holes
The one that sets fractured bones
The one that wraps a body in
the bark of the valkala and severs the limbs
The one meant for the ~~torture and killing~~ of deserters

—Vivek Narayanan

Queen of Cups

this old house is never cold, never quiet. moon-milk
splashes on the pebble roof. we sigh-roll off the hair-filled
mattress, pad to the unclad panes and imbibe the light

until we're drunk on our galaxies' proffering. we
know nothing of unstitched shadows or dark corners.
the fortune teller two towns south bids us sit, flips the

Queen of Cups. tunnels through its sundry meanings, sprinkles
sugar over the brightest parts. we humor them: smile,
present photos of infants we haven't birthed, wearing

pastel onesies with pastel woolen socks someone else
lovingly knitted. no, we can't mother. but we do
nurture. watch us—bumping elbows at the neighborhood

coffee shop, spilling our steaming black brew on a white-
collared wrist, eyes connecting. old-fashioned. the fortune
teller cannot see beyond the cards, is deaf to the

ancient thrum-thrumming in the air. we are old-fashioned.
we are fashioned from the old. rootless and without a
god-figure to tap our consciousness. we are rough-tongued,

sleek and star-dusted, a leonine vessel seeking
warmth. watch us—extending a wick-ignited candle,
inviting our new polestar to collect the dripping

wax on their exploring fingertips. how they hiss with
pleasure, ache for the flame to lap their marrow. yesss. we
promise them eternal love—of course we do! we, too,

yearn for this blessed heat, for the eloquent discourse that
precedes it: the mapping of bones beneath quivering
skin, the whisper of blades in motion, the rush of synced

energies. how much remains unknown to the cutter
of this deck. we tilt our chin at the Queen of Cups; a
measure of truth resides in her image, after all:

how we need filling, and how eagerly they offer
their unflexed limbs, untangled strands, salivating tongues.
we lick them—our barely contained lioness chuffing

with satisfaction, purring with pride. crank the heat to
its highest setting, listen to flame talking with hewn
bones, cartilage, viscera. such conversations warm

this old house—the discharging of gasses, combustion
of what remains. my lovers' dialogue does not cease
with the lowered flame. we mix their ashes with clay, mold

them into their spirit beast, feel their new skin adjust
to their boneless frame, saturating the love within
us. the fortune teller trusts anyone who calls up

the Queen of Cups. but—should we fault them? if they're drawn to
this old house with its pebble roof and vibrating walls?
are they wrong to embrace our fate? see this ram, this wolf,

this bull? they're hungering for the sickle in our stars,
our crescent promise, twinkling in the moon-milk above.
how could we starve them? we are leo. we are the Queen

of Cups, fashioned from the old. we know the importance
of preserving threads—true connections continue to
feed the soul, even long after the body is dead.

—Crystal Sidell

The River God Dreams of Death By Water

角田川もっと古びよ時鳥
Sumidagawa motto furubi yo hototogisu

—Kobayashi Issa

i. *The Upper Course & the rising light*

Cumulus cities topple in this heat

tumble-down ruins
better left unnamed

a conspiracy of blue
masks the stars

information afloat
on this ill wind

rises

against the flow of time

echoing

backwards

The absence of water
distills Our spirit
spills Our form

through these dry rocks
through this cracked earth

Creatures dwell within Us
hide in the fissures

in the formation
of thought itself

these stone triads speak of Us
in their ancient tongues

telling Our broken tales
of death and water

You rake over a chalky soil
rivers once ran through this
spirited and alive

circling in spirals seeking
dry wells and dusty beds
spun faster and ever deeper

But your thoughts are spiderwebs

—vibrations on a string
holding the memories of your lives
like somber flies trapped—

attached to life
at the world's four corners
tenuous & barely visible

Recognition goes straight down
to the shriveled root of things

the lattice below the surface
builds light and life

holds your secret wish
to wrap time
in silken threads

The bird of time
unspools its blood song
late into the night

like paper cranes
awhirl in midair

these brief moments
shed the burdens
of a body

in thrall to the shadows
lurking unseen

buffeting you
through dust
and darkness

to transcend the power
heal the damage

But a storm will break
when the thunder speaks

a sudden waterfall
to hide your thoughts
from yourselves

you cannot hear what you think
cannot speak what you must
the water dissolves your words

Take a stone
throw it into the river

see the ripples widening
to the edge

happiness is that moment
in time and space
enclosed like a secret garden

But so is hell:

the lotus root inhabits
just a patch of dirt
in an empty courtyard

four walls caked in mud

Some say your world
may end in flood

some say from the fire
that emits from within

but the moon still rises
leaves a light feather
for your pillow

a halo as wide as the sky

For *here* is the passage
that leads into madness

all the way down
to where the bodies lay
even your own

—and the river sees it all

Like sunken libraries
We are flooded
with memory:

falling *sakura*
trees of pain

a bone moon reflected
on the silent water

In wave upon wave
the words ripple

subside

fold you back to the implicate order
become real

as a dream becomes flesh

ii. *The Lower Course & the falling shadow*

The unlived life
is more examined
than your real one.
Things you meant to say,
dreams you meant to do
—but never did—
weigh heavy on your heart;
divergent streams narrow,
currents split apart,

as imagined fates itch
like phantom limbs.
You mourn the time
lost in this isolation,
the tears dried on
your pillow long ago,
but an ache remains
like a shadow
in the corner.
Some of you will call this
a living poem,
its verses built
from the ground up,
branching and blooming
like a sakura tree;
some of you will call this
an awakening,
a release from singing
your blood songs to the deaf;
some of you will call this
an infinite library
full of boundless chambers,
a tower built to heaven,
rooms branching outward
until reaching itself again
—a journey in leaving
that is never complete
and never meant to end;
some of you will call this
a world without Nature,
unrcal and unfathomable
with its figments and fragments
and objects of doom;
and some of you will
call this a river—still—
flowing and swirling,
never repeating,
yet holding steady,

like the conscious mind
awakened
from its slumber,
rising and falling
with the tides.
So We turn together
to that orange glow
in the trees
flowering against
the impossible blue,
that afternoon fade,
where slate colors all
and grey shadows fall
through trapdoors
in time and space;
We head with you
toward that perfect stop,
to that bend in the river
where everything
seems to change
and nothing
appears to end.

—Ryu Ando

The Second Funeral

The elderly woman sits
in quiet repose,
she can do no else,
as this was her last act before dying,
and yet she is not dead.
Her family has seen to it.
This great-grandmother,
this grandmother,
this mother, daughter, wife,
this fixture for generations,
may no longer have air in her lungs,
a heartbeat in her chest,
or that spark in her eye
her loved ones knew so well,
but she is alive still,
as long as her family refuses
to let go.

Today is her second funeral,
the first was eight months ago
when she stopped moving,
found in her favorite chair
by one of her grandchildren.
But it is the way of this village,
these people,
who have no fear of death,
in fact, they live for death,
it is the way of the ancestors.
Living here among the coffee trees
and the bougainvillea,
on stilted houses standing knee-deep
in a sea of thick green palm,
they welcome death as one would
an old friend.

Today the word has spread.
Today the villagers will come
and family from distant places.

Today the air will fill
with squealing pigs,
the bellow of water buffalo,
the rev of motorcycle vendors,
the catcalls from women
in tight dresses
selling cigarettes.
Today is the culmination
of eight months of receptions,
prayers and sitting with the family
at the dinner table,
the scent of formalin
masked by sandalwood.
Today is not the end
but only the next petal
in an ever-unfolding flower.

Today she will be moved
out of the home to one of the many
ancestral buildings that hug the hillside.
Later on, she will be moved
to a rice barn, where she will sit
and preside over the food
she cooked so well.
And, eventually,
she will be moved again,
to the funeral tower that
overlooks the ceremonial plain.
This process could take years,
if not decades, to evolve,
each time the distance growing
in gentle increments
to allow the bonds of love
to extend
into the afterlife.

—Kurt Newton

Spring, When I Met You (Spring, When I Woke)

I woke, melting ice my welcome
Back to this world
My skin danced around me
Dusty as an old snakeskin
And I shuddered under the snow
And shook and scratched
Until I could feel it giving
And above my skin the cold
Was giving way as sun
Softened what I knew was my grave
I crawled out of my old skin as I
Clawed my way to the light
Your last whispers still ringing in my head

Who are you whispering to now?
Do they know what you are?

You had no idea what I was
To be fair, neither did I
But now I remember my
Grandma's words about rot
And renewal and how some people are
Like flowers that bloom only once
And others can come again the next year
But she fell down dead the summer I turned
Twelve and I never found out the truth

So I was scared when you killed me
Was it fun for you making me love and then fear you?

I remember the ripeness of the mulch just laid
Down on the beds in the park thc day we met
You were walking, head down, earbuds in
And I smiled at you because you weren't looking
But you caught me anyway, the expression locked
Between us, like a rabbit held by a hawk
You were hunting me then, weren't you?
Only I didn't know it; I thought I discovered you

So handsome, the shy smile hiding the
Emptiness inside you—how dead you are inside

Dead enough to bury me here, in this same park
The mulch is even more pungent now that I'm twice alive

I'm naked and soon there may be a passerby who sees me
And I should care but I can smell bodies
There are more like me here
Well, not like me—they're only once-alives
But I can smell the decomposition
I've heard it's a unique smell and it's true
But there are variations, each one I find
Like tree-rings, like carbon dating
This one from last year, that one much older
How long have you been doing this?
And why is your scent layered on top of theirs
Over and over—you must come here so often
Had you just visited them the day we met?
The wind blows a familiar scent coming
Down the path—have I awakened on a day you visit
And won't you be surprised at what you'll find?

Snakes don't eat while they shed—like them, newly risen in a
Body that fully fits my rage, I'm hungry and you smell delicious

—Gerri Leen

The Thing About Stars

Heady drums and bird-trill flutes saturate
The clearing with music. We are gathered here tonight,
Friends, families, and neighbors,
United by this one night a year, the Festival of Stars.

The transient boy working on the repairs to my house
Has followed me to the forest. His giant-moon eyes devour
The scene around him, ever-curious.
Dancers swirl in the center of us, naked from the waist up,
Clad in skirts split at both sides, billowing anemones.
A folk dance as much as a war song,
And I shiver in the honeyed night.
The transient boy leans close to my chilled skin.
"What do stars have to do with anything?" he whispers.
I try to shush him, but the drums climb their fevered apex,
The flutes screech shrilly—wounded birds.
He isn't from the village, he doesn't know.
But tonight, he will.

Following the shift in music, the lissome, oiled dancers
In their spangled regalia extract the longswords
Hanging by their hips. The boy gasps by my side.
He must have thought them decorative,
When they are sharp as death's claws.
The dancers form a circular phalanx,
All of us from the village taking our cue to watch the sky.
The velour dark is writhing with bullet-holes of light.
"The stars," the boy says, "they're moving!"
The pinpricks against the sky bombinate,
Dislodging themselves from a firmament womb,
Shooting down, down into the glade with tails
Of fire and glimmerdust.

The boy by my side has grasped my hand,
Or maybe I grabbed his, absurd notion.
I've lived here for years, experienced many a Festival of Stars.
Not attending is unheard of. Stars fall once a year.
We fight them. We watch.
We win.

"Look," I tell the boy on tiptoes over the clamoring crowd.
In our center, warrior dancers surround fallen stars.
Their shape has yet to settle, amorphous limbs, humanoid
But for the viscous flow of light between ligaments.
The drums beat once, twice, three times.
The stars have no time to regroup nor get their bearings.
Dancers descend like richly plumed birds of prey.
Ours isn't the best vantage point, but I am well-versed
In what happens next.
I remember, every single part of it.

"The dancers train all year," I tell the boy
By my side, his nails quarrying moons
And other celestial bodies into my skin.
"The first thing dancers need to do is sever the limbs
So the stars fail to escape on foot,
Amputate their tails so they cannot return to the sky.
Then comes the slashing, the spilling of stardust
To feed the earth. Only a bit is best, it makes young saplings
Grow overnight. But let a star take root in village soil,
And it will stretch big and tall as an invasive baobab,
Strangling and demolishing everything it touches."

There's more, but my voice fails me,
My tongue a dust dune in my desert mouth.
The boy is weeping like a babe, or maybe I am.
I must hide, it isn't safe. I must cheer.
At the very least I must watch.
One of the stars from the nucleus knot of bodies
Locks eyes with me, emitting desperate, cosmic wails.
This star isn't turning arboreal like the rest of zir people,
Not taking root, but looking more human by the second.
It will not matter. It never does. These days, in these parts,
That's not enough to spare zir.

In my old village, I became neither tree nor plague
After my great, harrowing fall—
Just a child who grew into an adult living in fear and hiding.
Someone who attends the Festival of Stars each year,

Who watches the battered, dying stars,
Sees the pleas in their faces,
And swiftly looks away.

—Avra Margariti

Who Came from the Woods

The witch lives
in the woods and
waits for children,
they say; I got tired
of waiting, and moved
to town. I don't know
what monster lives
in the wood and
terrifies the children,
the last one was cut
into a thousand pieces
and thrown into the sea
by yet another Jack.

I married a man, solid, plain,
no magic needed—all I did
was braid my hair and smile
and not talk much to him.
And I made a child for myself,
handsome, sweet, out of his
hair and kisses
and teeth
and blood.
He's a proper growing child
becoming strong and bright
for all that his father's dull and loud.

The more my son grows tall,
his father wanes;
what's fair is fair, I say,
for his father said
he'd do anything, if he
could only see a boy child
an inheritance—
a lost tooth here,
a pricked thumb there
and never disturbing the nesting birds
in the rafters I brought inside by winter.

Some men are so desperate for a legacy
they don't care how you give it.
Come spring my boy will be to my elbows
and his father will be in the churchyard;
there's nothing I, or anyone
can do about the cough that's never gone away—
he traded his breath to live to see
his only dream fulfilled.

Well he's my son, now
mine, like the village is mine
shaped with time and worry and love.
Whatever's in the woods—
a monster, a mad thing
a magician driven to despair
by a debt with the devil—
my boy won't be the one
who wanders out when the mushrooms bloom.
The Host will not take my boy
for plucking strange flowers
or eating odd fruits.
He'll know his stories, and he'll know
the safest place for witches is right here
inside the stone walls, thank you,
selling scrumpy in the town square on Tuesdays.

Hush, darling, hush;
it will be quiet soon.
By equinox nothing will give you bad dreams anymore
soon, nobody will make you scared
or say that secrets will come out.
Soon it will be just you, me,
and the Martinmas birds
singing.

—Lev Mirov

Acknowledgments

Rasha Abdulhadi • "The Dead Palestinian Father" • *Anathema: Spec from the Margins* 15
Angela Acosta • "The Optics of Space Travel" • *Eye to the Telescope* 43
Angela Acosta • "Regarding the Memory of Earth" • *Radon Journal* 1
Angela Acosta • "Tamales on Mars" • *The Sprawl Mag,* October
Linda D. Addison • "Fracking-lution" • *Hybrid: Misfits, Monsters and Other Phenomena,* eds. Donald Armfield & Maxwell I. Gold (Hybrid Sequence Media)
Madhur Anand • "Mind Compression" • *Parasitic Oscillations* (Random House)
Colleen Anderson • "Machine (r)Evolution" • *Radon Journal* 2
Ryu Ando • "The River God Dreams of Death By Water" • *Abyss & Apex* 84
Kathy Bailey • "New Planet" • *Dreams and Nightmares* 122
Ariana Benson • "Black Pastoral: On Mars" • *Paranoid Tree* 17
Ruth Berman • "Werewolves in Space" • *Dreams and Nightmares* 121
Bruce Boston • "Strange Progeny" • *Hybrid: Misfits, Monsters and Other Phenomena,* eds. Donald Armfield & Maxwell I. Gold (Hybrid Sequence Media)
Rebecca Buchanan • "The Bone Tree" • *Not a Princess, but (Yes) There was a Pea, and Other Fairy Tales to Foment Revolution* (Jackanapes Press)
Rebecca Buchanan • "Matches" • *Not a Princess, but (Yes) There was a Pea, and Other Fairy Tales to Foment Revolution* (Jackanapes Press)
Sarah Cannavo • "Corvidae" • *Liquid Imagination* 50
Priya Chand • "Field Notes from the Anthropocene" • *Nightmare Magazine* 116
Carolyn Clink • "Necklace" • *Frost Zone Zine* 6
Jennifer Crow • "Harold and the Blood-Red Crayon" • *Star*Line* 45.1
Madalena Daleziou • "My Great-Grandmother's House" • *The Deadlands* 11
Deborah L. Davitt • "Blå Jungfrun" • *Strange Horizons,* September 26
Deborah L. Davitt • "Debris" • *The Avenue,* May 18
FJ Doucet • "Medea leaves behind a letter" • *Star*Line* 45.1
Melissa Ridley Elmes • "What the Old Woman Knows" • *Listen to Her UNF,* March 23
Jeannine Hall Gailey • "Cassandra as Climate Scientist" • *California Quarterly* 48:4
Maxwell I. Gold • "Mouth of Mirrors" • *Seize the Press,* June 14
Alan Ira Gordon • "Pittsburgh Temporal Transfer Station" • *Star*Line* 45.2
Amelia Gorman • "The Gargoyle Watches the Rains End" • *The Gargoylicon: Imaginings and Images of the Gargoyle in Literature and Art,* ed. Frank Coffman (Mind's Eye Publications)
Vince Gotera • "Old Soldier, New Love" • *Eye To The Telescope* 45
Sarah Grey • "Biophilia" • *Strange Horizons,* Fund Drive

Sarah Grey • "Bitch Moon" • *Nightmare Magazine* 118

Jordan Hirsch • "We Don't Always Have to Toss Her in the Deep End" • *The Future Fire* 62

Akua Lezli Hope • "Igbo Landing II" • *Black Fire—This Time,* ed. Kim McMillon (Aquarius Press)

Beatrice Winifred Iker • "Georgia Clay Blood" • *Fantasy Magazine* 80

Pedro Iniguez • "The Epidemic of Shrink-Ray-Gun Violence Plaguing Our Schools Must End" • *Star*Line* 45.3

Herb Kauderer • "ex-lovers & other ghosts" • *Cold & Crisp* 518

Pankaj Khemka • "Leda Goes to the Doctor" • *Carmina Magazine,* September

David C. Kopaska-Merkel & Kendall Evans • "Monitors" • *Star*Line* 45.1

Angel Leal • "The Machines Had Accepted Me For So Long" • *Radon Journal* 2

Nicole J. LeBoeuf • "On the Limitations of Photographic Evidence in Fairyland" • *Eternal Haunted Summer,* Summer Solstice

Mary Soon Lee • "Jingwei Tries to Fill Up the Sea" • *Uncanny Magazine* 45

Mary Soon Lee • "What Electrons Read" • *Simultaneous Times* 31

Mary Soon Lee • "What Wolves Read" • *Uppagus* 54

Gerri Leen • "Living in Rubble" • *Eccentric Orbits* 3, ed. Wendy Van Camp (Dimensionfold Publishing)

Gerri Leen • "Spring, When I Met You (Spring, When I Woke)" • *Dreams and Nightmares* 121

Sandra Lindow • "Intergalactic Baba Yaga" • *Dreams and Nightmares* 122

John C. Mannone • "A Creation Myth" • *Songs of Eretz,* Spring

Avra Margariti • "Herbaceous Citadel" • *The Fairy Tale Magazine,* January 4

Avra Margariti • "The Thing About Stars" • *The Saint of Witches* (Weasel Press)

Elizabeth R. McClellan • "Sabbatical Somewhere Warm" • *Star*Line* 45.4

Lev Mirov • "Who Came from the Woods" • *Strange Horizons,* January 3

Lee Murray • "Status Transcript" • *A Woman Unbecoming,* eds. Rachel A. Brune & Carol Gyzander (Crone Girls Press)

Vivek Narayanan • "From 'Poem without Beginning or End'" • *Poetry* 220

Kurt Newton • "The Second Funeral" • *Synkroniciti* 4:1

Eva Papasoulioti • "Petrichor" • *Utopia Science Fiction,* April/May

Max Pasakorn • "field notes from an investigation into the self" • *Strange Horizons,* August 29

Terese Mason Pierre • "In Stock Images of the Future, Everything is White" • *Uncanny* 46

John Reinhart • "Laws of Exponents" • **NewMyths.com** 59

Anna Remennik • "Please Hold" • **NewMyths.com** 58

Silvatiicus Riddle • "Exulansis" • *Liquid Imagination* 51

Marsheila Rockwell • "EMDR" • *Unnerving Magazine* 17

Marsheila Rockwell • "A Spell for Winning Your Personal Injury Lawsuit" • *Dreams and Nightmares* 120

Ryfkah • "The Long Night" • *Eccentric Orbits* 3, ed. Wendy Van Camp (Dimensionfold Publishing)

Lauren Scharhag • "Interdimensional Border Town" • *Unlikely Stories,* August

Crystal Sidell • "Queen of Cups" • *The Magazine of Fantasy & Science Fiction,* November/December

Marge Simon • "Raft of the Medusa" • *Silver Blade* 53

Alfonsina Storni, trans. Brittany Hause • "Lines to a Martian" ("Palabras a un habitante de Marte" • *Ocre* [Editorial Babel: Buenos Aires, 1925]) • *Asimov's Science Fiction,* November/December

Nwuguru Chidiebere Sullivan • "Gosh, It's Too Beautiful to Exist Briefly in a Parallel Planet" • *Strange Horizons,* November 21

Alyza Taguilaso • "Time Skip" • *The Deadlands* 16

Gretchen Tessmer • "Shipwrecked" • *The Deadlands* 12

Lisa Timpf • "First Contact" • *Eye to the Telescope* 44

Marie Vibbert • "If I Were Human" • *Star*Line* 45.2

Rebecca Bratten Weiss • "The Watcher on the Wall" • *Reckoning* 6

Shannon Connor Winward • "Near the end, your mother tells you she's been seeing someone" • SFPA Poetry Contest

G. E. Woods • "How to Skin Your Wolf" • *Strange Horizons,* December 19

Stephanie M. Wytovich • "Dinner Plans with Baba Yaga" • *Into the Forest: Tales of the Baba Yaga,* ed. Lindy Ryan (Black Spot Books)

2023 Longlisted Poems

Short Poems (102 poems nominated)

After the Quest is Over • Lisa Timpf • *Eye to the Telescope* 46
Air Born • Brian U. Garrison • *Corvid Queen,* November 18
Angels • Frances Skene • *Polar Starlight* 6
Anima • Thomas Zimmerman • *Pages Literary Journal,* November 9
Animal House Speech • Dave Chandler • *failed haiku* 83
Anodized Titanium • Mary Soon Lee • *Eye to the Telescope* 44
Aswang Shaman Communing with Diwata for the First Time • Vince Gotera • *Eye to the Telescope* 46
Australopithecus • Jessica Lucci • *How Can I Steal A Purse*
bathroom chatter • Matteo L. Cerilli • *Augur* 5.2
Beneath Everything The Future Still Exists • Maggie Chirdo • *Little Blue Marble: Warmer Worlds,* ed. Katrina Archer (Ganache Media)
The Best Ambassadors • Adele Gardner • *Felis Futura: An Anthology of Future Cats,* ed. CB Droege (Manawaker Studio)
Big Brother, Little Brother, and the Sea • Geneve Flynn • *Space & Time Magazine* 142
Blond Dude in a Laundromat • Mary Turzillo • *Best of 22* (Ohio Poetry Association)
Bone November • Sandra Kasturi • *The New Quarterly* 164
The Closest Traitor • Richard Magahiz • *Mobius: The Journal of Social Change* 33:2
Cursed • Lee Murray • *The Gargoylicon: Imaginings and Images of the Gargoyle in Literature and Art,* ed. Frank Coffman (Mind's Eye Publications)
Dark Neighborhood • Cindy O'Quinn • *Chiral Mad* 5
Dead in Orange Red • Jamal Hodge • *Monthly Musings,* May 9
Derelict Dreams • Bruce Boston • *Dreams and Nightmares* 121
Domestic Tranquility • Brian U. Garrison • *Radon Journal* 2
Doppelganger • James Arthur Anderson • *The Horror Zine,* Fall
Draft • Lavina Blossom • *Riddled with Arrows* 5.4
Equus Aloft • Sterling Warner • *Otoliths,* February
Helianthus • Eva Papasoulioti • *Solarpunk Magazine* 5
Hip Gnomes • PS Cottier • *AntipodeanSF* 291
Hockey Night in Canis Major • Gretchen Tessmer • *Kaleidotrope,* January
Home from the Wizard Wars • Lyri Ahnam • *Silver Blade* 54
The Honorable Iris C. Thaumantos, Presiding • Marsheila Rockwell • *Musings of the Muses,* eds. Heather & S. D. Vassallo (Brigids Gate Press)
How to Build an Altar • Angela Acosta • Halloween SFPA Reading

It's Not Utopian If There Are No Fat People • Jordan Hirsch • *Utopia Science Fiction,* December

A Lacing of Lavender • Carina Bissett • *HWA Poetry Showcase* IX

Letting Flowers Go • Alexander Etheridge • *Liquid Imagination* 52

Medusa • Akua Lezli Hope • *The New Verse News,* November 18

Medusa Bringing Her Children Back Home • *Salt* • Patreon

MetaGender Machine • Linda D. Addison • *Black Fire—This Time,* ed. Kim McMillon (Aquarius Press)

Mother Wicked • Dyani Sabin • *Strange Horizons,* February 28

Od's Bodkin • Colleen Anderson • *Space & Time Magazine* 142

Pluto is Not a Planet • Jamal Hodge • *SavagePlanets* 2:3

Pumpkin Ash and Cypress Knees • Katherine Quevedo • *Boudin: It Came from the Swamp*

Reasons Why You Can't Go Out to Play Alone • Victoria Nations • *HWA Poetry Showcase* IX

Sector 431B • Jamal Hodge • *SavagePlanets* 2:3

Skies over Carson Sink • Joshua Gage • *The Space Cadet Science Fiction Review* 1

Starfall • Melissa Ridley Elmes • *Spectral Realms* 16

Suburban Pitcher Plant, Sarracenia suburbiana • Jay Sturner • *Not One of Us* 69

Tasted Like Pork • Pankaj Khemka • *Ghostlight,* Fall

Terrible Truths • Linda D. Addison • *Daughter of Sarpedon: A Tempered Tales Collection,* eds. Heather & S. D. Vassallo (Brigids Gate Press)

Transformation Sequence • Stewart C. Baker • *JOURN-E,* September

The Veil • Anna Cates • *Otoliths,* February

Villagers • Tim Jones • *a fine line,* Autumn

Virgin Mary Meteorology • Patricia Gomes • *Muddy River Review,* Fall/Winter

Warming • Maria Zoccola • *Nightmare Magazine* 117

While Traveling Through Deep Space Aboard a Generation Ship • Terrie Leigh Relf • *The Drabbun Anthology,* eds. Francis W. Alexander & t. santitoro (Hiraeth Publishing)

Long Poems (70 poems nominated)

Ariadne Threads the Labyrinth • Adele Gardner • *Dreams and Nightmares* 120
Barn Cats • Adele Gardner • *NewMyths.com* 60
Beautiful • L. Marie Wood • *Under Her Skin,* eds. Lindy Ryan & Toni Miller (Black Spot Books)
The Birds Singing in the Rocks • Tristan Beiter • *Strange Horizons,* October 31
CONELRAD 1960 / COVID 2020 • T. D. Walker • *Fireside Fiction,* June
Crossing Over • Frank Coffman • *Liquid Imagination* 52
Crow Daughter • Gabriela Avelino • *Kaleidotrope,* Summer
Dark Matter Resume • Lorraine Schein • *A Coup of Owls* 8
Darkness • David E. Cowen • *The Hand That Wounds* (Weasel Press)
Drowning in This Sunken City • Deborah L. Davitt • *Strange Horizons,* July 3
Eidolon Tetratych • Frank Coffman • *Spectral Realms* 16
The First 100 Days • John Reinhart • *Star*Line* 45.2
A Fit Place to Live • David E. Cowen • *The Hand That Wounds* (Weasel Press)
For You Were Strangers in Egypt • Elizabeth R. McClellan • *Nightmare Magazine* 122
From the Ninth Brane • John Mannone • *Altered Reality Magazine,* February
The Frosty Voyage • Adele Gardner • *Eye to the Telescope* 46
Ghosting Our Steps • Luke Kernan • *Anthropology and Humanism* 47:2
Halloween Hearts (for Ray Bradbury) • Adele Gardner • *Halloween Hearts* (Jackanapes Press)
I am the Dragon • Elizabeth Fletcher • *Spaceports & Spidersilk,* October
If Houses Could Talk • Lori R. Lopez • *The Sirens Call* 59
In the Mirror's Grip • Jeff Young • *Eccentric Orbits* 3, ed. Wendy Van Camp (Dimensionfold Publishing)
In water • Soonest Nathaniel • Stephen A. DiBiase Poetry Prize 2022 Award Finalists
Like Thunder in My Head • Gerri Leen • *The Fairy Tale Magazine,* April
Lines of Non-Extension • Janis Anne Rader • *Consilience,* Autumn
Locks • Colleen Anderson • *Abyss & Apex* 84
A Message From Her Feline Self, Unborn, to Her Cousin, Whose Ancestors Were Once Wolves • Jessica Cho • *Fireside Magazine,* March
My Avian Daughter Devours Meteors • Alicia Hilton • *Ornithologiae,* ed. Mark Beech (Egaeus Press)
On Meeting Kari Solmundarson of Burnt Njal on a Ghost Ship • Amelia Gorman • *Nonbinary Review* 27

One Last Perfect Night • Jill Trade & Joshua St. Claire • *The Space Cadet Science Fiction Review* 1

Persephone in January: A Chant Royal • LindaAnn LoSchiavo • *Carmina Magazine,* March

Photographing Sirens • F. J. Bergmann • SFPA Poetry Contest

The Possession • Anna Cates • *Otoliths,* June

Questing Done Right: The Goblin Market • Elizabeth R. McClellan • *Eternal Haunted Summer,* Summer Solstice

Resilience • Francesca Gabrielle Hurtado • *Reckoning* 6

A Rounded Spell • Alessandro Manzetti • *Kubrick Rhapsody* (Independent Legions Publishing)

Seasonal Meat • Jamal Hodge • *Chiral Mad* 5

Team Enrollment • Herb Kauderer • *Scifaikuest,* November

Thirteen Ways to Know You Are a Witch • John C. Mannone • *Star*Line* 45.4

A Tribute to the Ferryman • Ngo Binh Anh Khoa • *Eternal Haunted Summer,* Winter Solstice

tzedek: the wild hunt • Elisheva Fox • *Strange Horizons,* November 7

Uncle Louie's Farm • Skip Leeds • *Pages Literary Journal,* August 18

Virginia Dare Brooks • Francis Wesley Alexander • *The Martian Wave* III:1

The Whippoorwill • Lori R. Lopez • *Spectral Realms* 16

Wings • Jordan Hirsch • *The Fairy Tale Magazine,* February

Zombie Pirate Ghost • Michael H. Payne • *Silver Blade* 54

Past Rhysling Award Winners

1978	Long	Gene Wolfe	"The Computer Iterates the Greater Trumps"
	Short	Duane Ackerson	"The Starman"
	(tie)	Sonya Dorman	"Corruption of Metals"
		Andrew Joron	"Asleep in the Arms of Mother Night"
1979	Long	Michael Bishop	"For the Lady of a Physicist"
	Short	Duane Ackerson	"Fatalities"
	(tie)	Steve Eng	"Storybooks and Treasure Maps"
1980	Long	Andrew Joron	"The Sonic Flowerfall of Primes"
	Short	Robert Frazier	"Encased in the Amber of Eternity"
	(tie)	Peter Payack	"The Migration of Darkness"
1981	Long	Thomas M. Disch	"On Science Fiction"
	Short	Ken Duffin	"Meeting Place"
1982	Long	Ursula K. Le Guin	"The Well of Baln"
	Short	Raymond DiZazzo	"On the Speed of Sight"
1983	Long	Adam Cornford	"Your Time and You: A Neoprole's Dating Guide"
	Short	Alan P. Lightman	"In Computers"
1984	Long	Joe Haldeman	"Saul's Death: Two Sestinas"
	Short	Helen Ehrlich	"Two Sonnets"
1985	Long	Siv Cedering	"Letter from Caroline Herschel (1750–1848)"
	Short	Bruce Boston	"For Spacers Snarled in the Hair of Comets"
1986	Long	Andrew Joron	"Shipwrecked on Destiny Five"
	Short	Susan Palwick	"The Neighbor's Wife"
1987	Long	W. Gregory Stewart	"Daedalus"
	Short	Jonathan V. Post	"Before the Big Bang: News from the Hubble Large Space Telescope"
	(tie)	John Calvin Rezmerski	"A Dream of Heredity"
1988	Long	Lucius Shepard	"White Trains"
	Short	Bruce Boston	"The Nightmare Collector"
	(tie)	Suzette Haden Elgin	"Rocky Road to Hoe"
1989	Long	Bruce Boston	"In the Darkened Hours"
	(tie)	John M. Ford	"Winter Solstice, Camelot Station"
	Short	Robert Frazier	"Salinity"
1990	Long	Patrick McKinnon	"dear spacemen"
	Short	G. Sutton Breiding	"Epitaph for Dreams"
1991	Long	David Memmott	"The Aging Cryonicist in the Arms of His Mistress Contemplates the Survival of the Species While the Phoenix Is Consumed by Fire"
	Short	Joe Haldeman	"Eighteen Years Old, October Eleventh"

1992	Long	W. Gregory Stewart	"the button and what you know"
	Short	David Lunde	"Song of the Martian Cricket"
1993	Long	William J. Daciuk	"To Be from Earth"
	Short	Jane Yolen	"Will"
1994	Long	W. Gregory Stewart & Robert Frazier	"Basement Flats: Redefining the Burgess Shale"
	Short	Bruce Boston	"Spacer's Compass"
	(tie)	Jeff VanderMeer	"Flight Is for Those Who Have Not Yet Crossed Over"
1995	Long	David Lunde	"Pilot, Pilot"
	Short	Dan Raphael	"Skin of Glass"
1996	Long	Margaret B. Simon	"Variants of the Obsolete"
	Short	Bruce Boston	"Future Present: A Lesson in Expectation"
1997	Long	Terry A. Garey	"Spotting UFOs While Canning Tomatoes"
	Short	W. Gregory Stewart	"Day Omega"
1998	Long	Laurel Winter	"why goldfish shouldn't use power tools"
	Short	John Grey	"Explaining Frankenstein to His Mother"
1999	Long	Bruce Boston	"Confessions of a Body Thief"
	Short	Laurel Winter	"egg horror poem"
2000	Long	Geoffrey A. Landis	"Christmas (after we all get time machines)"
	Short	Rebecca Marjesdatter	"Grimoire"
2001	Long	Joe Haldeman	"January Fires"
	Short	Bruce Boston	"My Wife Returns as She Would Have It"
2002	Long	Lawrence Schimel	"How to Make a Human"
	Short	William John Watkins	"We Die as Angels"
2003	Long	Charles Saplak and Mike Allen	"Epochs in Exile: A Fantasy Trilogy"
	(tie)	Sonya Taaffe	"Matlacihuatl's Gift"
	Short	Ruth Berman	"Potherb Gardening"
2004	Long	Theodora Goss	"Octavia Is Lost in the Hall of Masks"
	Short	Roger Dutcher	"Just Distance"
2005	Long	Tim Pratt	"Soul Searching"
	Short	Greg Beatty	"No Ruined Lunar City"
2006	Long	Kendall Evans & David C. Kopaska-Merkel	"The Tin Men"
	Short	Mike Allen	"The Strip Search"
2007	Long	Mike Allen	"The Journey to Kailash"
	Short	Rich Ristow	"The Graven Idol's Godheart"
2008	Long	Catherynne M. Valente	"The Seven Devils of Central California"
	Short	F. J. Bergmann	"Eating Light"

2009	Long	Geoffrey A. Landis	"Search"
	Short	Amal El-Mohtar	"Song for an Ancient City"
2010	Long	Kendall Evans & Samantha Henderson	"In the Astronaut Asylum"
	Short	Ann K. Schwader	"To Theia"
2011	Long	C. S. E. Cooney	"The Sea King's Second Bride"
	Short	Amal El-Mohtar	"Peach-Creamed Honey"
2012	Long	Megan Arkenberg	"The Curator Speaks in the Department of Dead Languages"
	Short	Shira Lipkin	"The Library, After"
2013	Long	Andrew Robbert Sutton	"Into Flight"
	Short	Terry Garey	"The Cat Star"
2014	Long	Mary Soon Lee	"Interregnum"
	Short	Amal El-Mohtar	"Turning the Leaves"
2015	Long	F. J. Bergmann	"100 Reasons to Have Sex with an Alien"
	Short	Marge Simon	"Shutdown"
2016	Long	Krysada Phounsiri	"It Begins With A Haunting"
	(tie)	Ann K. Schwader	"Keziah"
	Short	Ruth Berman	"Time Travel Vocabulary Problems"
2017	Long	Theodora Goss	"Rose Child"
	Short	Marge Simon	"George Tecumseh Sherman's Ghosts"
2018	Long	Neil Gaiman	"The Mushroom Hunters"
	Short	Mary Soon Lee	"Advice to a Six-Year-Old"
2019	Long	Sarah Tolmie	"Ursula Le Guin in the Underworld"
	Short	Beth Cato	"After Her Brother Ripped the Heads from Her Paper Dolls"
2020	Long	Rebecca Buchanan	"*Heliobacterium daphnephilum*"
	Short	Jessica J. Horowitz	"Taking, Keeping"
2021	Long	Jenny Blackford	"Eleven Exhibits in a Better Natural History Museum, London"
	Short	Linda D. Addison	"Summer Time(lessness)"
2022	Long	Beth Cato	"The Bookstore"
	Short	Mary Soon Lee	"Confessions of a Spaceport AI"

For all past Rhysling winners, runners-up, and nominees, see **sfpoetry.com/ra/rhysarchive.html**

How to Join SFPA

SFPA members receive the quarterly *Star*Line,* filled with poetry, reviews, articles, and more; the annual *Rhysling Anthology;* and *Dwarf Stars,* an edited anthology of the best short-short speculative poetry of the previous year. Each member may nominate one short and one long poem for the *Rhysling Anthology* and then vote for the Rhysling Awards from the anthology. Members may nominate poems of 10 lines or fewer to the *Dwarf Stars* editor and vote for that award. SFPA also sponsors the Elgin Awards for speculative poetry chapbooks and full-length books, and an annual poetry contest. See **sfpoetry.com/join.html** for current information.

SFPA Membership—One Year	$15 • .pdf only
$50.00 • United States print (*Star*Line, Dwarf Stars, Rhysling Anthology*)	$35 • U.S.; *Star*Line* as .pdf, *Dwarf Stars* & *Rhysling* as print
$75.00 • Canada	$55 • Canada
$80.00 • Mexico	$55 • Mexico
$90.00 • Overseas	$65 • Overseas

Five Years	$67.50 • .pdf only
$225 • United States print (*Star*Line, Dwarf Stars, Rhysling Anthology)*	$157.50 • U.S.; *Star*Line* as .pdf, *Dwarf Stars* & *Rhysling* as print
$337.50 • Canada	$247.50 • Canada
$405 • Mexico	$247.50 • Mexico
$720 • Overseas	$292.50 • Overseas

Lifetime *Payable in 3 payments over 3 years.*	$300 • .pdf only

Failure to make all payments reverts to number of years paid.

All prices are in U.S. funds. Please pay online via PayPal to **SFPAtreasurer@gmail.com**.